K9 Explosive Detection

A Manual for Trainers

Ron Mistafa

Detselig Enterprises Ltd.

Calgary, Alberta, Canada

K9 Explosive Detection
© 1998 Ron Mistafa

Canadian Cataloguing in Publication Data

Mistafa, Ron, 1950-
K9 explosive detection

ISBN 1-55059-161-4

1. Police Dogs—Training. I. Title. II. Title: Canine explosive detection.
HV8025.M57 1998   636.7'0886   C98-910104-5

Detselig Enterprises Ltd.
210-1220 Kensington Rd. N.W.
Calgary, Alberta T2N 3P5
Phone: (403) 283-0900/Fax: (403) 283-6947
e-mail: temeron@telusplanet.net
www.temerondetselig.com

Detselig Enterprises Ltd. appreciates the financial support for our 1998 publishing program, provided by Canadian Heritage and other sources.

Printed in Canada

ISBN 1-55059-161-4

SAN 115-0324

Cover design by Dean Macdonald.

TABLE OF CONTENTS

Introduction

This book was written to help those departments who do not yet have an Explosive Detection Dog, or who are not completely satisfied with their present system of Training Standards.

This book is not "the answer," but is more a series of helpful hints to set your unit on its way to more meaningful training and confidence. It places a lot of emphasis on effective and efficient training, which in turn produces very confident Detection Teams who search with high degrees of EFFICIENCY, EFFECTIVENESS and SAFETY. This book is designed for the experienced handler or trainer, but can be easily followed by the beginner as well. However, as with any Dog Unit aspect, always train with someone who has a lot of experience or is an expert, especially in Explosive Detection.

What I found missing throughout North America is a Course Training Standard with a simplistic theory, broader training methods and a system that requires scenario training as 60% of the course. There are three important aspects for success:

1. Quality of the Dog
2. Quality of the Handler
3. What the Handler learns that is appropriate to the functions the team will be performing.

To better explain, I found that most departments spend little or no time choosing a suitable dog candidate, due to budget constraints or to the belief that any dog will do, and therefore will send their handler out to look for a candidate. This is where knowledge is crucial. A "Quality" dog will be quicker to learn the basics – to recognize scents – and therefore allow more valuable time for scenario training for the team. Second, both the handler and the dog must be suited to the work. Explosive Detection is the hardest training a handler will ever go through with a dog. So, be sure your handler candidate knows what he/she is in for. Third, the course itself – what knowledge is most appropriate to learn for success in the field?

Over 90% of the courses offered to handler teams spend much of the classroom time studying drives, character traits and instincts instead of "how to." Learning about drives, character traits and instincts may tell you why a dog does what he does, but it does not tell the handler "how to" respond to the information, which is more important. Therefore, you can see that the better the dog, the less time needs to be spent on basics. The better the handler, the quicker the dog team learns and the appropriate learned information helps create a more confident and efficient team.

Another reason for a lack of good Course Training Standards is that so much emphasis is being placed on hi-tech machines. So much financing has been put into these machines that we are seeing the proven tool (dogs) being pushed off to the side more and more. The dog's nose is taking second place to mechanical Explosive Vapor Detectors (EVDs) and x-ray machines. The demonstrations and training courses given by the companies who make these machines have allowed airports and security companies to put these tools into the hands of lower-paid and less motivated/experienced personnel. Highly skilled dog teams are being relied upon a lot less and are not being utilized as front-line technicians.

The approach today is to have security personnel highly visible, with as many metal detectors, explosive vapor detectors and x-ray units as possible to help "prevent incidents." This is the hi-tech proactive approach. This approach is justified to the public and to police department managers as saving time and money on:

- weeks of training
- veterinarian bills
- dog food
- vehicles and equipment

However, what is purposely not mentioned through all of this hype is the ineffectiveness of these machines and the people operating them.

Now that attention has been taken away from the dog and the handler, a Course Training Standard that covers effectiveness, efficiency and safety is extremely hard to find. Because of this, five weeks or less of Basic Training is geared only to the dogs' ability to recognize the scents and sit. Nothing more is given to the handler/dog team as a whole to create an extremely efficient searching team.

A Course Training Standard Manual should emphasize the importance of:

1. the quality of the dog suited for this type of work.
2. choices of Training Systems to suit the dog, with fewer resulting washouts.
3. Search Theory that emphasizes the importance of scenario training to help create an efficient and effective search team.

A well-trained Explosive Detection Team is far more effective and efficient than a vapor detection team by itself. However, if you use the machine and the dog/handler teams together, you have one incredible detection system.

Ron Mistafa

General

Overview and Statements

As an instructor, you should have a good grasp of task description (how to explain to handlers the how and why of their training), instructor centered statements (guidelines for the instructor) and learning objectives. For those of you who are beginners at this, it can be totally overwhelming and can distract you from your main goals. Whether or not you are training drug dogs, street dogs or, as in this case, explosives dogs, you have to have a game plan.

This is why I have designed this book as a Course Training Standard Manual. It is designed for someone with a lot of experience as a handler. As an instructor, you will have to, at some time in your career, show your supervisors that (1) you are able to create a game plan in the form of a Course Training Standard; (2) you are able to carry through with your game plan as a supervisor in charge of training dogs and handlers; and (3) you are able to train your department's unit in a step-by-step fashion and are able to back up any problems that do arise by using your course plan.

First, as an instructor, know your Task Description. As an instructor, the handlers you train must be familiar with the course objectives, procedures and individual requirements to gain full benefits from the course. It should be designed to set an atmosphere that encourages learning and to provide the candidates with an overview of the course.

This is all accomplished through your Instructor Centered Statement. As the trainer, you will familiarize the handlers with the course purpose, goals, procedures, equipment and syllabus. Last and most important are the Learning Objectives. You will be able to teach each handler to:

1. prepare explosives for hides;
2. set up scenarios for training sessions;
3. relate to the course syllabus;
4. understand course objectives and individual responsibility;
5. problem solve;
6. understand legal aspects;
7. work with other specialty units;
8. handle and store explosives; and
9. perform first-aid.

For those of you who are attempting to create a Certified Course Training Standard within your own department, it is extremely important that you have hard samples and visual aids for all aspects of this course, as well as reference hand-outs (that go into great detail and pertain to all aspects of the handlers' tasks). Have all of this in the form of a neat package. This is important for supervisors of Career Development and Training or at P.O.S.T.

Choosing Candidates

Candidates need to be self-motivated, have the ability to keep impeccable training/work records and to enjoy the rigors of weekly maintenance training.

In addition, you can also choose a handler who has a minimum of two years of street dog work, a handler who desires to be a specialist, which sometimes requires the handler look after and train a second dog. The desire to be a specialist, though, is most important.

Explosive detection work is probably the most tedious and specialized work of any dog unit and the handlers' desires and stamina to become fully involved with this specialty is extremely important.

With all of this at hand, your standard will provide your selected members with the skills and the knowledge necessary to operationally handle an Explosives Detection Dog.

Your standard is also designed to provide certification for successful course candidates and give outside members a wider choice of options for testing standards. It enables them to choose this course standard of testing for certification (name school) or ones similarly designed to the RCMP course standard of testing or able to meet the F.A.A. course standard of testing. The options are many.

Upon successful completion of this course, Explosive Detection Dog handlers will be able to:

a) search for, and find, hidden quantities of explosives in aircraft, luggage, buildings, vehicles (i.e., cars, buses, etc.), air terminals, commercial buildings and buried items using the scenting abilities of the dog;

b) prepare training aids and hides for training scenarios; and,

c) provide first-aid for dogs adversely affected by apparent ingestion of explosives.

Explosive Detection Dog Requirements

- May be an untrained dog or a regular patrol dog that has been on the street for a minimum of two years.
- Experienced with and socialized to varied environments.
- Strong prey, retrieval and play behaviors that make up their personalities.
- Neutral general behavior (not overly aggressive or excitable).
- Good physical endurance and agility.

The German shepherd is the most versatile of all police dogs. They not only make excellent street dogs, but they also make excellent explosive detector dogs. The German shepherd comes in various colors: black and tan is the most common, all black and sable.

The Malinois is fast becoming number one due to its versatility. However, more care has to be taken in the selection of these dogs for detection work. A qualified handler or trainer should do the selecting, as this is a tenacious breed. These dogs come in red, sable (dark and light), and a light red or brown.

The most popular breed for a specialty is the Labrador. The reason for its popularity is that in detecting on or near people, the Lab engenders more trust in people than Shepherds or Malinois, which have a more aggressive reputation. Labs come in yellow, black and chocolate.

● No previous special training.

The most successful breeds for explosive detection are German Shepherds, Malinois and Labradors. Other breeds have been used, but these breeds seem to show the most consistency and reliability for this type of work. These three breeds also are the most frequently used in police departments and perhaps the easiest to train of all breeds. The six points listed above are general things I look for in explosive detection dogs.

How to Choose Your Explosive Detection Dog

Either untrained or trained is all right for explosive detection work. Untrained, of course, is self-explanatory, but trained means a regular patrol dog that has been on the street for a minimum of two years or has been pretrained in explosives detection. Having a dual-purpose dog (street/explosive detection) is totally acceptable. Some will argue otherwise, especially where an explosives dog is concerned. Why? The argument I get seems to be generic. Handlers want their dogs' minds on one thing – explosives, not humans. The response I give is that when you are part of a S.W.A.T. team or Emergency Response Team, you do calls once or twice every other day, putting your stress level high, and then you go to court or do community relations work. Do you attend to all these functions as you would going through the door at a call – following the number one man in – or do you attend to these functions in accordance with the tasks at hand, i.e., giving evidence or a lecture? Answer: you work in tune with the task at hand. Dual-purpose dogs can also be in tune with the task at hand. With street dogs that are dual trained, we tend to find a lot of skeptics in the crowd who say that detection dogs should be single-purpose, especially explosive dogs. The fear is that they will become aggressive toward other people in the area of the work and become distracted. Nothing could be further from the truth. We are not giving enough credit to the dog. In fact, I have not seen any difference in people's attitude toward a green, single-purpose dog and a seasoned dual-purpose dog. It all depends on the quality of dog, the attitude of the handler and the training course. However, I have seen problems with dual-purpose dogs that are trained in *aggressive confirmation* for drugs. In this scenario, aggressive confirming dogs tend to become bored and agitated on long searches and start clawing and chewing at anything that they come across that has human scent. I have not seen this phenomena with *passive confirmation*, dual-purpose dogs. But in this case, we concern ourselves with only passive confirmation.

For those who wish to and have the luxury, training a single-purpose dog is just as fine as training a dual-purpose dog for those who cannot afford to purchase another dog and wish to train and use their street dog as an explosive detection dog. Those who question this style are unable to give the dog the ample credit it is due with respect to its ability to do two completely different tasks. A good handler has the ability to change and keep the dog thinking of the task at hand.

The other alternative in trained dogs is, of course, the pretrained explosives dog. Some or perhaps most departments avoid these dogs because the training does not meet their department or trainer's standards. Pretrained dogs are extremely valuable. They can be successfully trained to meet anyone's standards and they save valuable time. As long as the dog recognizes all scents, and all of the appropriate information regarding the dog's ability is forwarded to you, you can have great success. However, don't buy a dog based solely on VHS tapes of dogs working; these are useful preliminary shopping tools, but VHS tapes can be doctored to make the dogs look good. Always test the dog in person to be sure you're getting the right dog for your unit.

Testing a Dog's Personality

Varied Environments

For the trained dog, this is not a problem. Untrained dogs should be introduced to as many varied environments as possible and evaluated. Some of the things I put the dogs through are metal grate stairs, escalators, elevators, slippery floors of all types, tight places, etc. I do this first on-line, then off-line and during play mode (retrieve item/toy). What I look for (in green dogs especially) is their reactions and recovery times.

Reactions (to look for)

Of course the dog that pays no heed to environmental changes is the one you want. However, the dog that successfully works through all dilemmas or problems is perhaps the best. The reason is that dogs that successfully work through their problems and carry on with the task at hand on their own tend to be the dogs that are most dependable and become quick learners. They will display the same abilities during a call, where you do not have the luxury or time to go into training mode to fix a problem.

What I initially look for is how the dog(s) will react to the following:

- linoleum: single shade; dark or light colored
- linoleum: patterned with light or dark shades
- floors with a highly polished glaze; could be ceramic tile or hardwood floor
- concrete floors; painted or unpainted and glazed
- carpet

I have seen dogs during training have no problems at all on any type of floor covering. But what I have noticed is that some dogs may react to the same floor but with a different color or shades of colors. Why? I have no definitive answer to give you. The reason for this, I have been told, is that dogs have an inherent fear of walking on ice. However, everything I have seen regarding this issue has been inconsistent. I am not a big fan of drives and instincts to describe a dog's personality. If a dog is wary of walking on a slippery floor because it resembles an ice surface, then shouldn't all dogs be, because it is an inherent aspect? My answer is NO! Dogs are like humans. Some humans have problems walking on a slippery/icy surface too. Why? Because it is just the way we are. The same applies to dogs. This is why throughout this book you will read of a dog's "personality" or behavior, rather than its drives or instincts when I describe its abilities for this type of work. However, I do talk of a dog's drives to state what strengths it should have, but not to describe why it does not have these characteristics due to a lack of specific genetic qualities.

For those of you who do not agree with this, ask yourself what genetic or instinctual qualities make a super athlete. I believe dogs are what they are because that is how they are made up. Not all of them will become detector dogs and not all of them can become street dogs or dual-purpose dogs. Therefore, we have to pick the dogs because of their abilities and not because of drives that are supposedly inherent in all dogs.

As for the problems with the floors and inconsistencies of theories as to why dogs have problems, I feel the problems that dogs have with floors are problems of perception, although I am unable to prove or disprove this theory. Either way, it is a problem that most dogs can work through. Other places to look for reactions are on escalators, luggage conveyors at airports and see-through metal stairs. To overcome or prevent problems, in most cases, play "retrieve" on or in these areas and also utilize your obstacle course for a few minutes each workday.

Reaction/Recovery Time

Different floor surfaces (textured/patterned) seem to be the biggest and most consistent obstacles for dogs to overcome. Floors of different texture may not be a problem for some dogs to overcome. For many, it is the shade of color or the abstract pattern with one or two closely colored shades that is the problem. Regardless of the floor surface, most floor surfaces that cause the problems are usually found at the calls you will have to do. This is especially true at schools, stores and malls.

The following are some ideas that you can use to easily determine if your dog will successfully overcome its floor problems. When you realize that a problem does exist, but you are not sure just how great it is, here are some things I do that you can use. While you are using these systems, observe your dog and watch to see if is becoming comfortable in that particular situation by ignoring the environment that first caused the distress:

● Since you do not know how the dog will react, complete this first part off-line. This will allow you, the observer, to see all reactions, as well as see how quickly the dog is overcoming its problems, if any at all.

● Let the dog walk about on its own, watching what it avoids. Look for the things I mentioned earlier, i.e., type of slippery floor and color.

● When avoidance does arise, present the dog to the area and observe. The dog will be showing signs of severe stress if you are observing the following:
  ○ ears lying down;
  ○ heavy panting for no apparent reason;
  ○ head is continuously low to the floor;
  ○ tail is tight between the legs;
  ○ hugging the wall while it walks about;
  ○ has to be coaxed to move about while at the same time pays very little attention to you; and,
  ○ tries to get out of the room situation by leaving and escaping back to the car.

● If you are observing all of these, cut your losses and get another dog.

● Now if your dog is displaying, to a smaller degree, the wall hugging and tentative walking on the floor, then put the dog on-line and walk around. Praise the dog verbally and physically. This will give the dog some additional confidence from the handler. Do this until the dog is comfortable with you here.

Leaving the line on, throw the toy around and while staying stationary, get the dog to bring the toy back to you. Observe how long this process takes for the dog to totally ignore the floor.

● If this is an ongoing process with no improvement, then it may be something that you will have to become accustomed to for some time. In this case I would "wash" this dog too.

● However, if the process takes a few minutes to a couple of hours, and progresses each day to less and less time to recover, then this dog is a keeper.

Patience is a virtue that you will come to appreciate in this work.

Strong Prey, Retrieval/Play Behaviors

These are some of the most important aspects in choosing the ultimate Explosives Detector Dog. The strength of each dog's desire to search for its hidden toy will dictate the dog's work ethics.

The basis for Explosives Detector Dog training relies on strong PREY, RETRIEVAL and PLAY behavioral characteristics that make up the dog's personality. These behaviors form a necessary part of the dog's personality in the wild that allows the dog to seek and capture prey for food and then return it to the den. After satisfying itself, the dog would then play with other members of the pack for enjoyment, as with humans.

Similarly, it is this strong personality that is used in the Explosive Detector Dog – to search and find a familiar substance (explosives), then bring or attempt to bring (or point out) the "booty" to his master. Play is positive, fun and used as a reward and motivator. The stronger the personality, the more aggressive the dog will be towards accomplishing this task. The dog will overcome difficult obstacles. Completing the retrieval exercises becomes more important than the distractions.

Testing Observations

Training in familiar environments can mask weak personalities. Training a dog to perform a routine in an environment which is comfortable to the dog can cause the tester to observe confidence or desire that may not be that strong. To get a truer assessment of the dog, the tester should change the routine of the dog and vary as many of the testing locations as possible. A dog's true colors should appear. A dog with a weak personality for an Explosives Detector Dog, as prescribed by these Course Standards, is easily distracted from the task at hand. This is where VHS tapes of a dog can be deceiving.

Let me give you an example of just how important it is to test a Detector Dog candidate. One of the most frustrating dogs I have tested for detection work is the Labrador. You will see how familiarity of environment, while testing a dog, can be deceiving. Most of the labs I get to choose from are of the working (hunting) lines. So when owners show me just how zany these dogs are to find and return the thrown item (now remember, this is all done outside on flat ground, high grass, in brush and so on), I then take this same dog to an industrial building to change the environment and observe how this high-driven, outside-playing dog will react.

The majority of these dogs wash at this point. When dogs wash out here it is usually because they fail to chase the ball. They choose not to chase the toy because they choose to check out the environment instead. The distractions are so overwhelming that the toy becomes secondary. This is totally opposite from the outside testing. The differences can be night and day.

I don't totally believe that this has to do with a lack of socialization. I have raised lab pups and have done nothing with them except feed them and play fetch with a wide range of different toys. Then, at the age of nine months, I have taken the pups to the Calgary International Airport during peak hours and played with them. The assessment – excellent.

So here you have dogs that have not been introduced to aircraft noise, rushing passengers, moving luggage conveyor belts, etc.; yet, these pups totally ignored all of these environmental distractions and paid total attention to only the toy.

I have my views on so-called socialization theories, in which I believe in part, but overall, I believe in simplistic techniques, which I believe I have begun to develop with good success. Therefore, be careful in your assessments of these dogs, be it a pup or a full-grown dog. One of the things I do, and I suggest others do the same, is to test, socialize (handler contact) and work with the dogs for 60 days before purchasing. The reason for this is that a majority of the failures make themselves known between 40 and 60 days. This is a long period of time to, first of all, put a lot of work into a dog and secondly, pay for something that doesn't work out.

Relevant tests that possibly demonstrate the soundness of the dog's qualitative behaviors are as follows:

1. Play with objects of different textures (e.g., wood, plastic, metal). The more readily the dog retrieves these different textured objects with enthusiasm, the better.

2. Play retrieval by throwing objects into different environments (e.g., hedges, tables, small rooms, slippery floors, fields, car interiors, under vehicles, noisy places, etc.). The less deterred the dog, the better.

3. Put an article in a place inaccessible, but in full view of the dog. The best place is on the other side of a chain link fence. Send the dog to retrieve it. The longer the dog works at trying to get under the fence, over the fence, or around the fence without any encouragement to retrieve the ball, the better.

4. The following test is the one I like best overall, because it can be done anywhere and it shows the dog's true searching desire and ability. Hide a toy in a place out of sight, but semi-accessible to the dog (best done inside). The best toy item for this, I find, is the kong, because a piece of the explosive (wrapper) can be placed inside it. The odor of the explosive is then related to the toy. After it is in place, have the handler let the dog search for the toy. The dog can be encouraged.

OBSERVE:

- Does the dog leave the area? Most do because they do not know how to search. If it does leave the area, but appears to be looking for the toy with zeal, this is acceptable. Just encourage the dog back to the area and observe.

- If the dog wants to find the toy but is having difficulty finding the zone, then direct the dog's nose to an area below the hide so that the scent cone can then be worked upward by the dog (remember, scent falls).

  Watch closely when the dog gets its nose into the cone of scent.

- Is the dog taking notice?

● Is the dog working it out?
● Is the dog needing encouragement?
● Is the dog leaving it altogether?

The foremost thing to look for here is indifference to the scent cone and continually leaving it. If this is the case, then be wary. However, if the dog is working very hard, but appears not to understand the mechanics of searching the cone, keep working with the dog until it gets the toy, then repeat. Remember, use lots of praise.

You can do this in different areas to see if the dog deviates. Once again, the more successful the dog is with the least amount of encouragement from its handler, the better the dog will be for detection work.

5. The other method I like to use is similar to the *Landespolizeischule fur Diensthundfuhrer* (State School for Police Dog Handlers) system in Stukenbrock, West Germany. What is needed for this type of testing? I suggest:

● a large open area, perhaps with a hill;
● a small stream (if a stream is not available a large bucket or several buckets of cool water may be used); and
● the dog's favorite toy.

If a hill is available, thrown the ball up the hill, so the dog has a lot of resistance when going after the toy. Keep playing this retrieval game until the dog is tiring. When the dog is tiring, and it should be thirsty from the long retrieval exercise, throw the retrieved object beyond a place where the dog has an opportunity to have a drink of water (e.g., past a bucket of water or across a small stream). If the dog retrieves without drinking that is BEST . . . obviously Retrieval is the priority with the dog.

If the dog stops for a drink on the way back after gaining possession of the article, that is still good. If the dog drinks instead of playing the game (and his thirst is not unreasonable) self-indulgence is the dog's priority. A dog should not be accepted if it is disinterested, dull, easily distracted or distressed by any common environment. These tests can also be used to evaluate a dog with no formal training, but it is preferable they be done using the dog's familiar handler. The locations used should be unfamiliar to the dog.

There are many tests that can be conducted with success; however, these systems seem to provide the higher percentage of successful explosive detector dogs.

6. Other observations to assess/watch for when testing an explosive dog are:

- "Not returning the retrieve toy back to the handler after each throw."

    If you have a dog with a high interest in retrieving, but who does not want to give the toy up, plays keep-away or continues on with the toy in its mouth, investigating other areas and totally oblivious to the handler, then you have a dog that is going to be a handful. Dogs with these traits usually take longer to train and usually frustrate the handler and trainer. Although tougher to train, the dog can be trained to perform quite well. It just takes a little longer.

- "Retrieving the toy, then dropping it to investigate something else."

    A dog that displays these tendencies usually will not make a good detection dog. The overriding factor here is that the dog puts priority in distractions (new changes to the environment) instead of playing and focusing on the prey/toy item. Playing with the toy should be the primary focus for the dog.

- Dogs can show well when tested outside and inside and still fail. How? After you have determined that the dog has potential, hide the toy on the wall, forklift, etc. Tease the dog while he sees you hide it in various places. While on-line, take the dog and let the dog find the toy on its own. Encourage the dog when its nose is at the hide to recover the toy.

    Several negative things may occur at this time. Firstly, the dog may not make any attempt to search/recover the toy while on-line. Secondly, the dog may attempt to search/recover the toy at first, then as soon as it is commanded to "SIT," the dog may stop looking for the toy altogether. Thirdly, the dog may stick to the handler by looking up to the handler's face. This third point is what I have found Labradors do a lot. This is, I believe, attributed to stress and the dog's submissiveness towards the handler due to the tone of commands, etc. Trying to encourage the dog to eventually overcome this particular problem(s) will usually take more time than any department has to offer. I would have to say that dogs such as these are "wash outs."

"Rank" Dogs

A dog that is rank (aggressive) towards the handler (usually Malinois but can be German Shepherds and Labradors) should only be used by an experienced handler. I do not recommend that a dog with this personality be given to a green handler. Why? Every time the handler has to give the dog a correction (verbal or leash), chances are the handler will end up in the Emergency Department of the local hospital. Airport work calls for a dog that socially accepts other people without confrontation. However, these types of dogs can still make good explosive detection dogs. A limit should be set by the trainer as to the degree of rank a dog displays towards the handler. There is no way you will be able to train an explosives dog and feel comfortable if the dog has a high degree of rank. As the trainer, if you feel that you should release the dog due to too much rank, even though it is good, RELEASE it. You will not regret the decision.

Possessive Dogs

Dogs that refuse to release can also pose aggressive problems. A dog that brings the toy back but refuses to release the toy to the handler is a problem for the beginning stages of training. Why? It is during the beginning stages that fast, repetitive sets are most important, but is not possible if the handler has to continually fight with the dog to release the toy. Also, handlers find themselves in the "jaws" of a dilemma because some dogs bite.

There are solutions, but success depends upon the handler's ability and sometimes strength. The most used system to make a dog release a toy is through pain. However, it has been my experience that this is a short-term solution and eventually causes the dog to avoid the handler. Things that I have done to more or less reduce the time spent trying to get the dog to release the toy is by choosing a toy that can be easily taken from the dog. The extra large Kong works well. The size of the Kong allows me to get my gloved hand inside the mouth and makes the dog release. To prevent the dog from jumping up at your arm as you pull the Kong away from the dog (at which time the dog has gone from sitting in front to jumping up and tagging your arm) I get the dog to release and then cup both of my gloved hands over the Kong and hold it at my belt buckle. At the start, the dog does try to mouth the hands and toy. But as he does this, hold your hands in place and command the dog to SIT, then HEEL. As the dog goes to the HEEL, place the toy in a pocket or pouch and resume the training exercise. Using this method teaches a dog a retrieve, release and heal routine.

The second way, which I use the most, is the hollowed out plastic rods. These are long enough and slippery enough that as soon as the dog comes to a SIT in front of me, I just grab the toy and slide it out hard and fast. The dog cannot hold onto it when it is extracted in this fashion. The less confrontation during the early stages of training the better. Have someone with experience pick out a dog for the handler if the trainer is inexperienced.

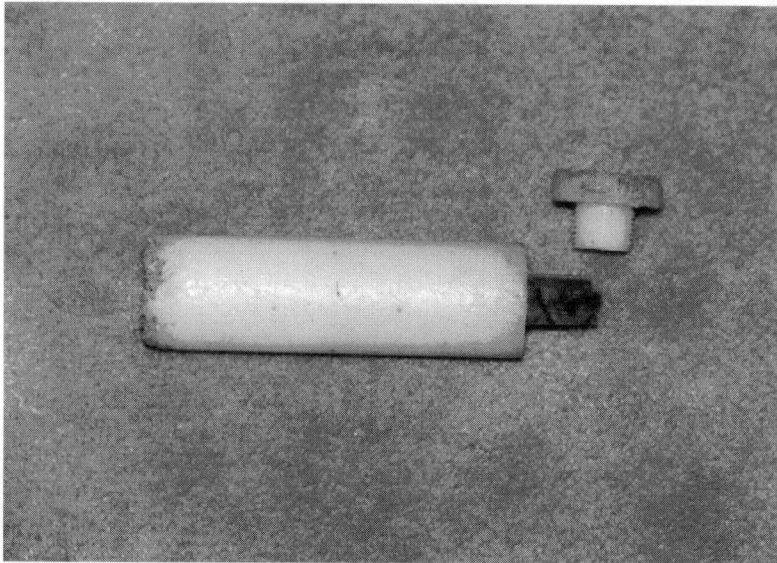

These toys are best at 6 to 8 inches long, and a diameter of 1½ to 2 inches, depending on the size of the dog. You can make screw tops for both ends, and make extras as the ends get chewed first. Make the scent holes large enough to allow dirt to fall out and to ensure a continuous scent is emitted.

Training Methods

Training is based on the concept that a dog learns by repetitions of exercises properly conceived and for which it receives positive reinforcement. During training the orders of progression and attention should be given to:

- acquainting the dog with the specified scents and ensuring physical conditioning of the dog;
- familiarization with environments subject to explosives searches;
- building the intensity and sureness of the dog's find response;
- developing the handler's ability to read the dog's indications; and,
- developing effective, efficient and safe search patterns.

Over the years I have been fortunate to have used various techniques for training detection dogs. With explosive detection, I lean more towards European techniques. Much of what I have learned has been taught to me by Brian Amm, who was my trainer when I was a dog handler with The City of Calgary Police. Brian was taught in Germany. Since then, I have become acquainted with three distinct training systems and they are:

1. *Landespolizeischule fur Diensthundfuhrer*, Stukenbrock, West Germany.
2. Royal Canadian Mounted Police Dog Training Centre, Innisfail, Alberta, Canada.
3. Lackland Airforce Base (U.S.A.F.), Texas, U.S.A.

Although I do not use any of these systems *verbatim*, any one of these systems or a combination thereof will give you success. The Course Training Standard I put together uses a combination of these standards similar to all three of the above and their techniques.

1. The German System

The German System, as taught to me by Brian Amm, is a system of Play/Retrieve with a hollowed-out, non-toxic, plastic or hardwood toy filled with the explosives. (Two to three different types can be placed inside of one toy.) These toys are approximately 1¼" x 1½" in diameter by 6" to 8" long, with small holes drilled into the toy to allow the scent of the explosive (or drug) easily escape for the dog to indicate.

Training begins by throwing these hollowed toys for the dog and playing fetch. The fetch game continues and grows to throwing the toy(s) under cars, in piles of junk, high grass, etc. It then progresses to placing the toy(s) high and low along walls where the dog can easily find them, begins to learn to do a search pattern and easily extracts them when found.

When the dog accomplishes this aspect with success, then the dog is commanded to SIT as soon as its nose comes up to the toy. When the dog reaches this stage with success, the toy(s) are replaced with real explosives placed high and low along the wall. As soon as the dog's nose comes close to the explosive, it is commanded to SIT and then the dog is given the plastic toy that he searched for earlier as a reward.

2. Royal Canadian Mounted Police System

The system used by the Royal Canadian Mounted Police (RCMP) is similar. However, toys are not used. Instead the dog starts off with explosives. Upon reaching the explosive, the dog is commanded to SIT and is rewarded with a leather piece or cloth to play tug-of-war with. It should be noted that with the RCMP system, the dogs chosen have to be extremely talented, because before the dogs get into explosives training, they first have to go through training as patrol dogs. This is an extremely tough course for dog and handler because both are trained for two different aspects during the same course. The RCMP use a "Level" system throughout the dog's training. I combine all or nothing. For me, either the dog does it all (luggage, buildings, autos, etc.) or it does not pass.

3. Lackland Airforce Base System

Lackland begins their training by using a series of cardboard (or wooden) boxes approximately 8" x 8" x 12" in size with a hole large enough for the dog to place its nose inside.

Do not make the holes any larger as you will find out how easy it is for your dog to get its head stuck in the box. If the head becomes stuck, you will have to take the box apart to get the dog's head out.

Hide box with spice jars inside.

This system begins by bringing the dog to a box that contains an explosive and as soon as the dog sticks its nose inside, it is commanded to SIT. Then, the dog is rewarded. This system then progresses to a series of boxes placed in strategic areas of a room, i.e., each corner of a room, in a row, and high and low, etc. There is much more to Lackland's Training Standard than what I mention. However, this system by itself or in combination with the other two systems should be considered extremely valuable to all police departments throughout North America.

I am sure throughout the years, through success and failures, all of us who are involved in training explosives dogs have taken bits and pieces of someone else's standard and picked out the best of these pieces that suited our own training needs. This is what is done here.

For starters, I really like Lackland's system of box training and the German System of a toy that has enclosed multi-types of explosives. What I did with my standard was that I used spice containers that were slotted to hold small amounts of eight different kinds of spices. I put different types of explosives into the slots, e.g., slot 1, 2 and 3 would have DM-12, slot 4, 5 and 6 would have C-4 or all the slots would be filled with smokeless powder. Use whatever is needed at the time. I worked the boxes with the dog until it was comfortable and sat at each box hide while I continued to walk on. The explosives would then be taken out and individually hidden. On the other hand, if I had a dog that was naturally driven to search, then I would go directly into searching for the explosives, implementing easy hides and getting the dog to SIT right from the start.

Taking everything into account, I use the Box Training together with the RCMP system, while utilizing the multi-explosives aid of the German system. However, in some cases I also utilize single explosive hides in the boxes. I do this for the emulsions and perchlorates. Why? Due to the softer or pasty content of these explosives and others of the same consistency, it is just too messy after you cut apart these explosives. (These are sticks that are 12" to 14" long and will not fit into the boxes.)

Either make boxes that fit the explosives or place the explosives by themselves on regular searches. Whichever of these systems you wish to use will be fine. However, as I stated earlier, I choose to use the system that will suit the dog's personality. That is what makes this Course Training Standard so unique and versatile. There is no one system, no one answer. There is only a good trainer who is able to get inside of the dog's head to see ahead of time which road the dog should take as opposed to the road it wants to take and being able to make the handler feel positive no matter how many mistakes are made or how bad things may be going.

4. D.D.S.I. System

Up until now all of our attention has been focused on testing. The testing to date was completed to assess whether or not the candidates are suitable for explosives detection. The dogs were also assessed to determine their degree of desire to work (retrieve). With all of this in mind, we will now categorize the dog's desire on a scale of three range levels:

1. High Range
2. Mid Range

3. Low Range

Placing the dog into one of these ranges or in between two of these ranges will help you to determine which technique or combination of techniques will be used to train the dog. The ranges are self-explanatory and are all-encompassing. The dogs are rated either below or above a level or at a level. For example, a dog that is rated at the Low Range will either make it with an extreme amount of time and effort or will not make it at all. However, if you, as a result of your assessment, feel the dog is leaning more towards "Below the Low Range" level, then cut your losses and find another dog.

However, if the dog was rated above the Low Range level, (mid-way between the Low Range and the Mid Range), there is a chance that the dog can become a fair detector dog. Here again, effort and time will be essential. We also must realize that what we are observing with the fair-rated dog could be immaturity. Six months from now this dog may be an excellent detector dog.

The range levels where you will see the greatest amount of success without a great deal of time and effort is from the Mid Range Level to the High Range Level. Each dog is now rated and placed into its perspective range level. Now we must corroborate the range levels with training techniques.

It would be impossible for me to categorize all range levels to training techniques because each dog, with its own personality, can create an infinity of observations. However, I will give some examples for each range level to give you some idea of what I am talking about and to show how I approach some of these situations.

High Range Level Dogs

A dog would be placed at this level due to its strong desire to work and high retrieval personality. The dog did not stop looking for its toy when hidden and the dog was easily directed by hand and voice, I have determined that this dog will be searching off-line for an explosive within seven to ten days and be sitting at the hide. How can I be so sure? Because this dog wants to work. The dog enjoys the challenge, the work and the reward. A dog at this range level usually becomes bored with box training; hence, actual searches suit a dog such as this better.

This is how I would set my Training Plan for this dog:

A. Box Training

I would utilize four Hide Boxes (HB).

HB1 – TNT/N.G.

HB2 – PETNs and RDXs

HB3 – Perchlorates/Amm. Nit.

HB4 – Powders

Note: B means Box, e.g., B1=Box 1. These have no explosives inside.

Now, set out seven or eight wooden boxes all in a row. The sequence I start with is: HB1, B2, HB2, B4, HB3, B6, HB4. (This is just an example – trainers should vary the quantity of boxes and the sequence to suit the dog's skill level and interest.) The first HB should have the TNT/N.G. explosive because they have the strongest odors. The second HB will have the Perchlorates/Amm. Nit., the third HB will have the PETN/RDX inside and the fourth HB will have the Powders (see illustration).

Note: Have two types of Hide Boxes: HBs for specific multi-grouped explosives, and HBs for singular explosives.

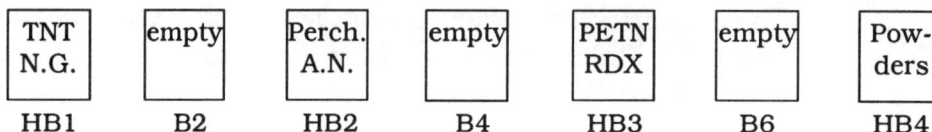

TNT N.G.	empty	Perch. A.N.	empty	PETN RDX	empty	Pow-ders
HB1	B2	HB2	B4	HB3	B6	HB4

B. Box Training/Empty Rooms

In the same training area, locate an area where there is a series of empty rooms (small 10' x 10' offices). A series of four to six rooms would be ideal. In each room place an empty box except for the second or third room. In one of these two rooms (your choice) an HB will be placed inside.

C. Box Training/Storage/Office Areas

In this area only two boxes will be utilized. Box One will be neutral while Box Two will be an HB. These boxes will be hidden in such a way that even though they are accessible to the dog, they will become part of the surrounding environment.

D. Scenario Training

All areas: offices, work areas, lockers, desks, garbage cans, luggage and vehicles.

E. Passenger Buses/Aircraft

In this section there is a direct training correlation between buses and aircraft.

I will now give a more in-depth account of the training for the High Range level, Sections A to E inclusive:

A. Box Training: "Find It Command"

We make up four HBs, each containing a specific group of explosives. We separate these explosives in order of the strength of their odors and contamination strengths. In other words, I put the TNT/N.G. into one box because their molecular build-up is the strongest and most odorous of all the explosives. We do not want to contaminate the other less odorous explosives (PETN/RDXs) with the overbearing TNT/N.G. explosives. The dog has to be able to locate each explosive based on its own makeup. I place the RDX/PETN together, the Perchlorates/Ammonium Nitrates in another box and Powders in the fourth box ready for the box training (Powders should be wrapped in nylons). I always try to have a minimum of eight boxes. However, it is okay to use a few more. I now place all of the boxes in a row, leaving a five to six foot space between each box. All of the HBs are in this row, utilizing all four explosive groups in the following sequence: HB1, B2, B3, HB2, B5, B6, HB3, B8, HB4.

Placing the more odorous explosives first gives the dog a very strong and easily smelled explosive to find first, which is then followed by very high/positive praise with a quick reward. The handler and the dog start a few feet away from HB1.

A sampling of explosives wrapped in nylons for hides.

I found that if the dog team starts too far away, the dog tends to run towards the boxes, running by the first one or two boxes without checking them. With the dog on line and in a sit position, have the handler move just ahead of the dog. Now have the handler command his dog to FIND IT (or similar), while at the same time tap the first box with his free hand.

Note: The handler should never hold the line tight. Hold the end of the leash only. If you find the handler is tripping over the line or the dog is getting wrapped around the handler's feet, then either have the handler hold the leash hand higher in the air or you may suggest a slightly shorter leash. The leash should be a maximum of eight feet and a minimum of six feet.

The handler must entice the dog to put its nose into each box through the opening. Spend only enough time to allow the dog to get its nose in and take a whiff, then quickly move ahead of the dog (while the dog's nose is still in the box) and begin tapping the next box with the free hand and giving a FIND IT command. With the first HB (first in the row), the handler has to be sure the dog gets a good whiff (count 1-2-3 seconds) and then command the dog to SIT. As a trainer you have several options to help speed things up. You can command the dog to SIT instead of the dog's handler. Why? It helps to ensure the dog does in fact get a good sniff and that the timing of the command to SIT was not done too quickly and not too late. It also helps to give green handlers a better concept of the timing aspect. Believe me, it works and you will not have to do it for long. But as the trainer, you will find that every once in a while you will have to command the dog to SIT for the handler because the handler is confused or missed the indication. Indications at this stage are usually a quick, downward jerk of the head, slowing down momentarily and placing its nose inside the HB. This can happen very fast and unless the handler observes this, the dog will continue onto the next box. Whatever the reason, never be afraid to make that decision. However, handlers learn the concept of timing very quickly.

Now remove the HB and replace it with another neutral box and place the Hide Box at the end of the row after HB4. Have the handler go back to the start and repeat the sequence (the dog must sit at each HB).

Note: Always have the handler reward the dog away from the hides; never near/into other hides. You never want the dog sticking its nose inside the HB while at the same time going after its toy/reward.

Your box sequence should now be: B1, B2, B3, HB2, B5, B6, HB3, B8, HB4, HB1. Repeat the sequence of boxes again (second round) making sure the handler gets his dog to place its nose into the openings of each box and moving in a smooth and steady fashion. Once the dog reaches HB2 the trainer should observe when the nose enters the box, count 1, 2, 3 and shout SIT. While the handler (green handler) praises the dog, the trainer can (as an option) throw the reward toy (ball/kong) at the dog. Once again, I will state (whether the handler or the trainer is throwing the ball/kong), throw the toy at the dog right after the count and while the praise is going on, but away from the other hides. At this stage, who throws the ball is not important.

This time you remove HB2, but DO NOT replace it with a neutral box (this is only done with HB1). Instead, remove HB2 completely out of the way (place it quite a distance away.) Now your sequence will be: B1, B2, B3, B4, B5, HB3, B7, HB4, HB1.

With the handler at the start (after a short play/praise) and the dog on leash, repeat this sequence. Sequence completed,

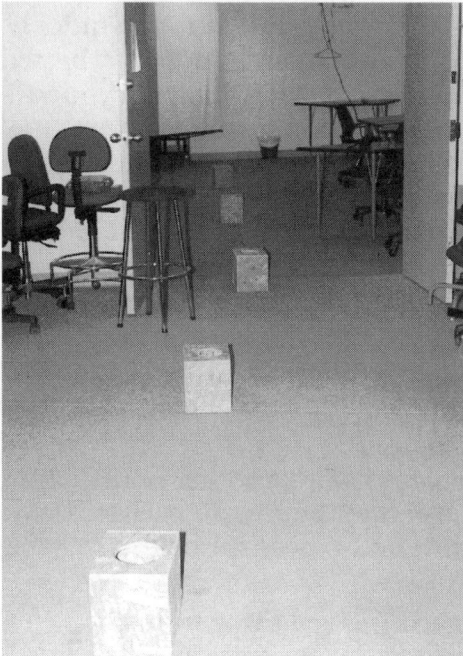

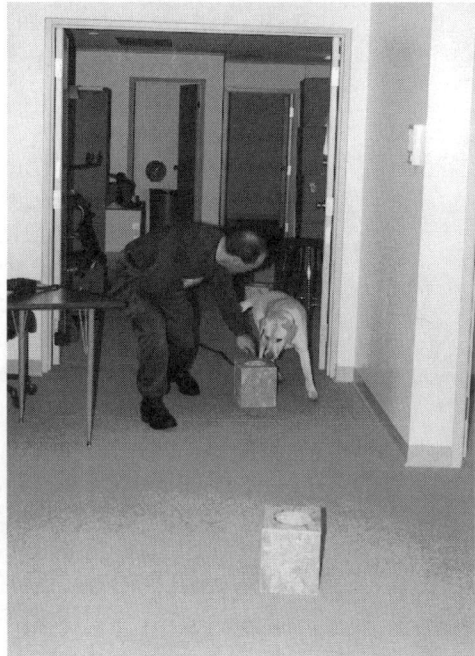

The handler directs the dog to each box. Only one box will have the hide to detect.

once again remove HB3 and place it away from the search area. The fourth set should now be B1, B2, B3, B4, B5, B6, HB4, HB1. Complete the row of boxes. Reward/praise at the hide. Take the Powders away. Your sequence should then be B1, B2, B3, B4, B5, B6, HB1. Complete the sequence for the fifth time.

DAY 1

I do this set (rotation of hide boxes) approximately five to six times during the first day. That is, the dog has searched the row of boxes five times, finding a total of five HBs (the TNT/NG was found twice). Repeating these sets five times during the first day means the dog has found/confirmed 25 HBs of different explosives altogether. The dog should be sitting comfortably on its own by the time it finds its fifth HB; however, because it is something new to the dog, it will forget or will from time to time remain standing because it is anticipating its reward/toy. This is not a big deal.

When the dog puts its nose inside the box with the hide, the handler commands the dog to sit.

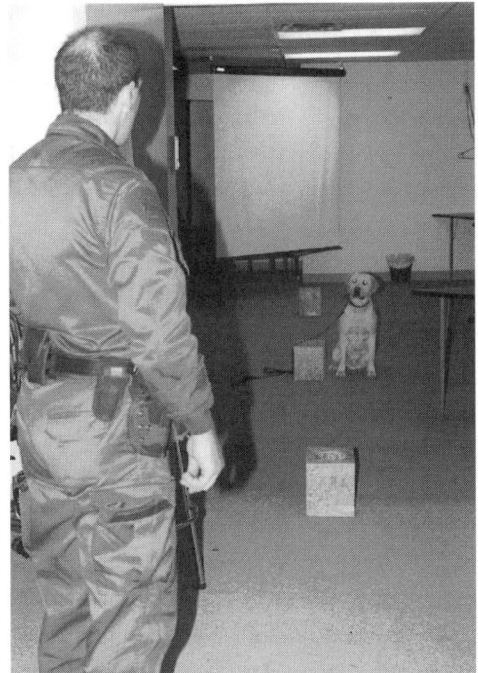

The dog must remain sitting at the hide box for a minimum of 10 seconds while the handler continues to the next box. The handler can then reward the dog. The time the dog must remain at the hide box will increase as training progresses.

DAY 2

I repeat day one, except now the handler can let the line drag. In other words, the handler now has to depend on his/her wits to make the dog sniff each box. Should the dog surge ahead, the handler can grab hold of the line by stepping on it or getting hold of it by hand, giving the dog a little tug and using verbal commands to remind the dog to slow down the pace and not to miss a box. But doing the sequence without hanging onto the line allows the dog to work independently, which it will be doing 90% of the time. Later on in the book you will learn why I do it this way.

DAY 3/4

Now reduce the number of boxes placed in a sequence. A total of five boxes in a row will be utilized. This will include the HB. Throughout the day, five sets of five searches will be completed. That will be 25 searches.

On the fourth day, six sets of five will be completed for a total of 30 searches. Setting up for this part of the training is simple. First, you have the same four HBs:

HB1 – TNT/N.G.

HB2 – RDX/PETN

HB3 – Perchlorates/Amm. Nit.

HB4 – Powders (Black/Smokeless)

On each of these two days, set the boxes in sequence as follows:

SET 1: B1, HB1, B3, B4, B5

Complete this set on-line. At the start, have the handler begin as the days before; trying to keep the pace steady and at a good speed. The handler should always be just ahead of the dog. With line in hand, the handler will command the dog to FIND IT. At this point, the handler should not have to tap the boxes with the free hand. A dog of this range level will create its own challenges, readily placing its nose into each box and sitting at the HB.

Note: From time to time the dog will hesitate to sit and remain standing. This is acceptable because, as do humans, dogs too have to repeat the exercises enough times before they become confident and at ease with their tasks.

The handler approaches Box 1 on line. The second box is HB1. As the handler approaches HB1, have him/her drop the line. Now remind the handler to keep walking one to three steps beyond HB1, always keeping the dog in sight. As soon as the dog puts its nose into HB1, have the handler count 1, 2, 3 SIT. Now a distance between the dog and the handler has been created. This ideal should be worked on time and time again to help create trust and comfort for the dog while it works at greater distances from the handler in the future. After the SIT the handler can reward the dog by throwing the toy/reward away from the boxes. The length of time the handler plays with the dog is the amount of time it takes the trainer to move HB1 into position #3 for the second Search.

Your sequence should now be: B1, B2, HB1, B4, B5. Now repeat the second search on-line at each of the first two boxes, but drop the line as they approach HB1. The handler should keep on walking approximately three steps further, always facing the dog and stopping. As soon as the dog has its nose inside the box, count 1, 2, 3 SIT. Then throw the toy and praise. The trainer should move HB1 to position #4 for Search 3. (The distance from the dog will increase when the trainer feels the dog is comfortable.)

Your sequence should now be: B1, B2, B3, HB1, B5. Repeat FIND IT search. Trainer now moves HB1 to position #5 for Search 4, so your sequence reads: B1, B2, B3, B4, HB1. Repeat FIND IT search. Trainer once again moves HB1 to position #1 for Search 5. The sequence should be: HB1, B2, B3, B4, B5. Repeat FIND IT search for the last time for Set #1. Five Sets of five Searches = 25 Searches.

However, during the 5th Search, have the handler drop the line just as the team approaches HB1. Now watch closely – the dog may become confused at HB1 and not stop and sit as the handler continues to walk the few steps beyond. This is a common occurrence and will only be solved through repeated searches where the HB is replaced back to position one every other search. Practice this, but do not let it concern you unless these box searches are part of your certification. The more this is practiced, the better the dog will become. When these sets are being completed, the best situation for a training class is to have a minimum of two dogs. This allows for several things:

1. Gives each dog a rest period.
2. Allows other handlers to observe other teams working.
3. Gives the trainer a chance to hold impromptu question/answer sessions with the handlers. This third point is, in my opinion, a most valuable tool.

Depending on how many dogs are in a class, each dog must complete Set 1 before the first dog is ready to do Set 2. Also, as the handler completes each Search, the other handlers in the class should help the trainer move the boxes so that the trainer can put more time into focusing on the handler and the dog currently doing the Searches. This is a team effort.

SET 2 : B1, HB2, B3, B4, B5

If a handler is still having problems with the dog surging ahead, then repeat Set 2 and each of the other Searches as prescribed for Set 1 until the dog is comfortable with the concept. Otherwise, complete Set 2 with the line dragging alongside the dog. Complete the five HB Searches as was done in Set 1.

SET 3 : B1, HB3, B3, B4, B5

Complete Set 3 without a leash on the dog. The handler/dog team should have repeated these searches enough times that both walk in unison down the row of boxes at a good tempo. Complete the five HB searches as was done in Sets 1 and 2.

SET 4 : B1, HB4, B3, B4, B5

Same Search format as done in Sets 1, 2 and 3.

SETS 5 and/or 6: Any HB can be used here.

For these, repeat Sets and try to use the explosives in the HBs that appear to you to be causing problems for your dog, as most dogs do have a problem explosive – one that they appear to take longer to confirm is present. However, as a trainer, it will be your choice. Also, the trainer should determine by the fourth day if the handler/dog team requires one or two more days of box training.

What is being accomplished during these four days is:

1. Recognizing all of the explosive groups in a short time. Some experts state that Explosive Detector Dogs should never be trained on multi-grouped explosives. Training should be accomplished with one explosive at a time. However, I have done it both ways and found no difference, just as I find no difference in dual purpose (Explosive/Street) dogs. Your training should suit the dog's abilities, not an ideal. Training the dog with multi-grouped explosives quickens the training process.

2. Very quickly, through many speedy repetitions, it teaches the dog to confirm by sitting at the explosives group. Once a trainer has accomplished this, begin the next step.

DAY 5/6

During these two days Box Training is still utilized but with some differences. First, the HBs will now have only one explosive instead of multi-groups of explosives; and second, four to six small rooms (approximately 12' x 12' or so) are used for this process as well. These rooms should be empty or at least partially empty. For example if we have four empty rooms, you could place a neutral box in each of the first three rooms. A box should be placed along a different wall or in a different corner of each room. The fourth room will have an HB. Before each box/room Search begins, gather all of the explosives and separate them into each of their own HBs. For example, start off with one-half to one pound of Perchlorate, then DM-12, then Det. or Prima-Sheet, then C-4 and so on. Whatever numbers of explosives are available, they will now be used one at a time.

After you have chosen which explosive will be used, and before the room searches are started, set out five boxes in a row, one of which will contain the chosen explosive. The HB can be placed in any sequence desired. In the same manner as the day before, complete five repetitions with the row of boxes first. After each Search, the trainer moves the HB into whatever sequence desired. This Set should be completed briskly, to keep the dog's strong desire to search and have fun. (The handler can increase the distance from the dog each time the dog sits.) Now do the room searches.

Now the trainer can move the same HB into position in the fourth room. Have the handler place his dog into a sit position at the front of the first door. When ready, the handler can command the dog to FIND IT. Remember that these first three rooms have three neutral boxes (one box per room) in different locations. But there are also light switches and plug-ins on the wall. These room searches are the beginning of systematic searches. The dog will enter the room and quickly sniff the box when it is found; however, the handler can have the dog sniff each of the plug-ins and light switches. This is done by having the handler tap the plug-in or light switch with the fingers and at the same time saying FIND IT. As soon as the dog puts its nose on the object, praise the dog and move to the next wall object, repeating FIND IT, and to the next. Remember to praise the dog each time its nose is placed on the plugs or switches. Other objects on the wall can be checked also. What this does is teach the dog to investigate on its own. The more search repetitions, the more investigative the dog will become. Each room should be completed quickly because there is not much for the dog to search. When the first room is completed, move quickly to the second room, then to the third and fourth. When the fourth room is reached, have the handler remain at the door until the dog confirms the HB. Why remain at the door?

FIRST: This training teaches the handler to remain at the door, watching for what the dog misses; and,

SECOND: In this case, standing back gives the handler the opportunity to observe a change in the dog's posture – from search mode to find mode to confirm mode.

The dog's change in posture is very noticeable and the ability to recognize these changes is extremely important. The handler must be able to recognize if the dog has found an explosive hide, food or some other strong smelling odor(s). Handlers can easily become confused if they are unable to tell these differences from an early stage. As the training goes on, the handler will become an old hand at recognizing the signs of his/her dog.

Repeat these Searches for the same explosive at least four more times, always changing the room where you place the HB. The combined time for a Set of Searches should be no more than 30 minutes. Therefore, being able to complete all of the explosives 10 times each/day is not a problem.

The system is especially good because if you use all of the explosives (approximately seven) during the course of the day, each dog will have completed approximately 70 searches. Also, you will find that the handler will not have to enter each room at all. Each handler will only have to stand in the doorway and observe while the dog does all of the work on its own. I recommend that these sets of searches be completed during these two days. A seasoned trainer will be able to recognize when the dog is doing extremely well and may elect to go directly to Box Searches/Storage/Office Areas. However, the more repetitions completed the more competent the dog becomes.

DAY 7/8 Box Searches/Storage/Office Areas

Until now, the dog has searched for multi-grouped explosives and individual explosives in a matter of days. The dog investigated box after box and just prior to Day 7/8, began to sit on his own, confirming a hide.

Still using boxes, this is the beginning stage of teaching the dog to search busy or cluttered environments on its own. In this case, the only boxes to be used will be one neutral box and one HB with one explosive of choice. Any cluttered area is fine as long as the boxes can be integrated into the surrounding environment so that the boxes are not obvious. A place that comes to mind is a courier service or a supply storage room where there are a lot of boxes. An area of 25' x 25' is adequate. Place the boxes (one on each side of the room) on their sides, so that the openings are facing the dog. The reason for this is that the boxes will be placed within other boxes. Also, place one box at floor height and the other three to four feet off the floor.

Note: A little trick for everyone training detector dogs that are searching and finding the hides very well but are still having problems grasping the SIT confirmation, place the HBs higher up so that the dog has to reach for it. What happens here is that when the dog stretches upward to sniff the HB it becomes very easy for the dog to come to a sit by virtue of its upright/downward momentum. It works very well. Eventually the dog will only stretch part way up the scent cone and sit quickly.

Getting back to our search area, send your dog on an off-line FIND IT search. Do your inside searches from left to right (I'll explain why later). After you send the dog in for the first time, it may be a little wild and will usually go right by the boxes without even taking note of them because the dog is so busy sniffing everything else. However, as a trainer, this first search is going to be very important to the dog and for the handler. First, after the dog has been sent in, make sure the handler watches what the dog has already searched, but remembers what has not been searched. The one thing I teach is that you must trust your dog. What tires out a dog more than anything is a handler who constantly makes the dog search over and over again the areas that have been searched by the dog and cleared. So from the start, I have always had the handler remember all the areas not searched by the dog. Once the dog has done a quick "Cursory Search," have the handler call the dog back to begin a "Systematic Search." (Making the handler remember what is not searched while at the same time keeping his/her eyes on the dog takes a lot of practice.)

Starting left to right and at the lowest position (floor level), have the handler direct the dog with his/her hand and command the dog to FIND IT. As the dog has its nose low and is working, the handler should now move two or three steps down and as soon as the dog has finished working that area, have the handler repeat the FIND IT sequence, except this time direct the dog to investigate higher. While the dog works this area, once again the handler should move down the line and as soon as the dog finishes working the high section, the handler again directs the dog to a lower area and commands it to FIND IT. What you have is a Zig-Zag or a Low/High Search Pattern. There are three reasons for using this Search Pattern Style:

1. It allows the dog to cross the Scent Cone.
2. It prevents the handler/dog team from having to search the area again. The entire area is covered in the Low/High Search Pattern.
3. Through many repetitions the dog learns to search in an independent and thorough pattern.

Place several boxes high and low in a room. This helps dogs overcome any confusion over changes in search environment. You can start with boxes exposed, then hide them, then hide the explosive alone, so the dog doesn't key on the boxes, but on the scent of explosives.

As the dog becomes more efficient and effective in its searches, the handler will only have to recall the dog to search what has not yet been searched. In most cases, the dog may miss only one or two spots. As the dog approaches the area where the neutral box is located, carry on as usual and direct the dog by hand to the general area of the box, but not at the box. Remember, you want the dog to search for the box and find it on its own. Finding the box on its own, even though it is an empty box, is very important. Finding the box leaves an imprint on the dog that the fun here is looking for the boxes. The dog is now beginning to realize the purpose to this training. As the dog places its nose into the empty box, the handler should already be moving down to the next position. When the dog lifts its nose out of the box, then the handler can command the dog to FIND IT.

When the handler nears the area where the HB is, have the handler watch the dog closely. When the handler sees the dog hit the Scent Cone, the dog should be quickly and only momentarily praised. As soon as it hits the box and puts its nose inside, the handler should count quickly 1-2-3 then SIT, then reward quickly this first time. Take the dog away and play. This is all part of recognizing the changes in the dog's posture.

Now the trainer can replace the HB with the neutral box (and move the HB to another area of the room). Why? When the handler sends the dog in for the second search, I guarantee that nine times out of ten, the dog will go directly to the spot where the HB was. Dogs have great memory recall, so they will automatically go back to that rewarding spot. But now there is only an empty box.

Note: One of the greatest aspects of box training in this fashion is that now you are teaching the dog to search for the scent and not the box that holds it. The dog becomes fixated on the scent of the explosive.

Getting back to the search, let the dog go on its own to check the last HB spot. The dog will investigate the now neutral box. As soon as it is done, call the dog back to the start. Remember, search Left to Right and begin the Low/High Search Pattern until the area of the HB is neared. Same as the first search, have the handler stand back and observe the dog. Again the handler is observing the change in his/her dog's body language as it enters the Scent Cone. As soon as the dog places its nose inside the box, the handler can command the dog to SIT.

Complete each explosive search four to five times each in this area on Day 7. On Day 8 move to another similar search area, but without the boxes. Use only the explosive (half pound to one pound) for now because these are quick easy hides that do not require much Soak Time. The explosive can be placed inside of boxes, between boxes that are stacked and on the floor under pallets. This time complete two searches per explosive per area. The reason for this is the air will become heavily laden with explosive odor and may confuse the dog in its early learning stages.

Note: If more than three dogs are being trained at one time, have two separate areas for each explosive. This prevents the dogs that follow from being attracted to the hide area by the earlier dogs' saliva/scent. If two separate areas are not possible, then I would suggest one explosive per search per dog. Then when the group is done the first set, remove the first explosive and put in another explosive in another part of the room. Leave the first hide area open so it airs out because the dog will go there first as we discussed earlier. If you do run into a shortage of training space then use what you have wisely.

By Day 7 the dog should be comfortable and not miss a hide, unless for some reason the scent is being drawn away. During these two days (Day 7 and 8) you will see a handler/dog team transforming into an efficient and effective detecting tool. Now the team is ready for Scenario Training, Passenger Buses and Aircraft.

Mid Range Level Dogs

This is the level at which most detector dog candidates will be evaluated. Dogs in this range fill the job description as adequately as High Range Level dogs:
- these dogs accept challenges;
- they accept direction from the handler;
- their work ethic is steady and extremely reliable;
- their desire to be rewarded for work accomplished is high; and

● due to their steady nature, these dogs seem to readily accept Box Training, i.e., they do not seem to become bored.

The factor that divides the dogs between these two range levels is intensity. Dogs in this range level do not work with intensity; they work with steady, focused desire. These dogs are steady in maturing and in developing. For all handlers, but especially the green handlers, these dogs are best suited. Following the training process as it progresses at this level seems to create better equipped handlers and extremely dependable dogs. Why? Due to their steady demeanor, these dogs seem to grow or mature with the program as it progresses. Handlers who train these dogs do have to work a little harder and a little longer to succeed, whereas the dogs at the High Range Level or the "Super Dogs" do more on their own in a shorter time. Hence these dogs actually produce a handler as a result of their super abilities instead of the handler producing a detector dog.

However, it is very intriguing to see which dog most handlers would pick. For me, the dog at the Mid Range Level and slightly higher is the one I would pick. Instead of seven to eight days to produce a dog familiar with the explosives and sitting comfortably as with the High Range Level dog, these dogs are usually take 14 to 18 days for the same results. The following is how I would set my training plan for the Mid Range Level dog:

A. Box Training

Firstly, utilize the same four Hide Boxes (HBs) mentioned earlier. Use all of the same sequences listed.

Note: Have two types of Hide Boxes – HBs for specific multi-grouped explosives and HBs for singular explosives.

B. Box Training/Empty Rooms

In the same training location, locate an area where there is a series of empty rooms (small 10' x 10' offices). A series of four to six rooms would be ideal. In each room place an empty box, except for the second or third room. In either the second or third room (your choice) an HB will be placed inside.

C. Box Training/Storage/Office Areas

In this area four boxes will be utilized. Three boxes will be neutral boxes, while one box will be the HB. These boxes will be hidden in such a way that even though they are accessible to the dog, they will become part of the surrounding environment.

D. Scenario Training

All areas used are offices, work areas, lockers, desks, garbage cans, luggage and vehicles.

E. Passenger Buses/Aircraft

In this section there is a direct correlation between buses and aircraft.

I will now give a more in-depth account of the training for the Mid Range Level dogs, Sections A to E inclusive:

A. Box Training: "Find It Command"

As with the High Range Level dogs, four HBs are made up, each containing a specific group of explosives. Stay with the same format, separating the explosive groups in order of the strength of their odors and contamination strengths. Try to use the minimum number of eight boxes – a constant through the stages for all range levels. The space between the boxes should also remain at a distance of five to six feet. All of the HBs are in this row, utilizing all four explosive groups. For the Mid Range Level dogs, I utilize this sequence of boxes in a row (B indicates neutral boxes): Set 1 - HB1, B2, HB2, B4, B5, HB3, B7, B8, B9, HB4, B11.

As with High Range Level dogs, the more odorous explosives are used first. This allows the dog to have a quicker find from a stronger and easily scented explosive. The difference with this sequence is that the dog gets a quicker reward because the first box is an HB. The reason for this is that these dogs are not as intense and you should therefore make the search task easier and not a high-speed challenge. Remember, these dogs seem to have more of a steady focus on their work without the exuberance. After each find, these dogs also should receive high praise and then quickly thereafter their reward toy.

The trainer should have the handler/dog team (dog on-line) start a few paces away from HB1 in a sit position. Now have the handler move just ahead of his dog at a smooth and steady pace. As the dog approaches the box, have the handler command the dog to FIND IT while at the same time tapping the box with the fingers of his/her free hand. When the dog places its nose inside of the box, have the handler drop the line and command the dog in a stern voice to SIT. Then a lot of praise followed by a quick reward.

Note: Once again a reminder – the handler should not hold the leash short or tight. Have the handler hold the leash at the end. However, if the line becomes tangled, have the handler hold the leash higher in the air or you may want to suggest to the handler to use a slightly shorter leash. The length of the leash should be a minimum of 6' to a maximum of 8'.

For the dogs that fall right on the Mid Range mark or slightly lower, the trainer can add some extra enticement for the dog. The trainer can use the dog's toy (ball/Kong) to artificially increase the dog's desire to hunt. There is a slight danger here in that we are now enticing the dog to search for its toy, whereby the smell of the explosive becomes secondary in importance. You must be able to reverse the order of importance. In other words, you must find the right time to stop using the toy as an enticement and turn the explosive into the primary target. The following is how I have accomplished this.

First, I can usually determine by the first or second set that the dog will require some extra encouragement. Without it the dog may sense a lack of purpose and begin to shut down by the end of the week.

Second, I obtain two or three of the same toy. I place a clean and identical toy into each box. The original toy that the dog usually chews is held by the trainer. With the handler and his dog at the start of the boxes, the trainer now teases the dog by showing or bouncing the toy (reward object) and pretending to place this toy into each of the HBs and neutral boxes. The trainer then hides the toy under his/her armpit or behind their back, out of sight and scent of the dog.

During this time the handler encourages his/her dog to FIND IT in an excited voice. Once the trainer is back at the start and standing off to the side of the team, the dog team can approach the HB with the toy/explosive.

Note: The trainer should be off to the side of the team so the toy can be thrown at the dog and away from the other HBs.

As the dog places its nose into the box, it will smell the toy and the explosives. Some dogs will SIT when commanded, at which time the trainer can throw the toy. However, in most cases the dog will become excited and frustrated at the same time and will either bark and paw at the box or just paw the box. Do not get frustrated, this is a natural way for the dog to react to the frustration of knowing and wanting its toy and because it is what it would normally do under normal play time situations. For the first set (set of HBs), the handler should FOOEY the dog from pawing at the box and encouraging it to FIND IT by putting its nose inside the box (The size of the opening becomes very important here.) Just as the dog starts to pull its nose out, the trainer can now throw the toy. The dogs will catch on fast in this range level. Remember, this is natural for the dog. We are not teaching the dog to dig for explosives. It is just the process at this level.

For the first set or even perhaps the first two sets, it will not be important for the dog to sit. It is more important that the dog keeps its tempo up while looking for the HBs. The main focus will be to increase the dog's tempo and for the handler to utilize the FOOEY command when the dog paws the HBs and praising the dog at the right times.

What will surprise most handlers is how quickly the dog learns. What handlers and trainers alike will find is that a large portion of the dogs will sit and look at the box because they are frustrated. When a trainer can see this coming, this will be one of the times when he/she can command the dog to SIT and then reward.

Note: Going back to the High Range Level dog, our training did not utilize a toy for encouragement, although I do not discourage it. Because of their gung-ho attitude and wanting the challenge, I found most of these dogs also will paw or try to pull the explosive out of the box with their mouth. But we stop this with a FOOEY, jerk of the chain and then the SIT command.

However, if the dog is still pawing the HBs by the time the third set arrives, then we can instill the FOOEY command and if you have to, a FOOEY with a quick jerk of the choker chain, followed quickly by a SIT command.

What we are trying to accomplish is to correct the unwanted actions, but praise and reward the appropriate actions. This process should only have to be applied for the first two sets in most cases.

As soon as the dog is rewarded, the trainer can remove the HB1 and put it at the end of the line after B11. The second Search for Set 1 should be B1, HB2, B3, B4, HB3, B6, B7, HB4, B9, B10, HB1. Repeat the sequence as before. However, the dog will have to search one neutral box first before it gets to HB2. Once again, entice the dog at the start. Repeat the exercise while the trainer makes observations of the dog and handler team. Once completed, remove HB2 completely. The sequence should now be B1, B2, B3, HB3, B5, B6, HB4, B8, B9, HB1.

Again, with the handler/dog team at the start, the trainer entices the dog by throwing/bouncing the toy in front of the dog and appearing to place the toy into each box while the handler is encouraging the dog. Now the dog has three neutral boxes to search before it gets to HB3. Remember, the handler should be trying to keep the tempo of the search at a high rate. By the time the dog "hits" the HB3 you will probably be seeing some positive changes. If not, don't get discouraged. Just keep going until you do. When HB3 is completed and the handler/dog team is away playing, the trainer removes HB3 completely. Your sequence should now be B1, B2, B3, B4, B5, HB4, B7, B8, HB1.

Repeat as the previous search. Now the dog has five neutral boxes to search before it comes to HB4. The trainer should be making mental notes of positive/negative changes. Once the handler/dog team is playing, the trainer can remove HB4 out of the way. The sequence of boxes should now be B1, B2, B3, B4, B5, B6, B7, HB1.

This time the trainer is to refrain from enticing the dog before the search. The handler should only play long enough for the trainer to take HB4 away. Now have the team get right into the search making sure the handler is enticing the dog with praise each time it places its nose inside of a neutral box. Remember there are now six neutral boxes to sniff. Trainers should be making observations of the dog's progress in order that a mental plan can be pictured for Set 2. Once completed, give the dog a rest. Discuss with the handlers what they observed.

Set 2 will have a slightly different sequence and be conducted in another manner. Remember, everything is done to suit the dog's personality. The sequence of Set 2 should be B1, HB1, B3, B4, HB2, B6, B7, B8, HB3, B10, HB4.

Note: Each HB will already have a clean toy inside or one will be placed inside after each HB is completed.

This time there will only be one enticement for the dog by the trainer. After the first search, the handler will be responsible for the dog's encouragement. Also for this set, as each HB is completed, remove them from the row. After the first and only enticement and the trainer is back at the start, the handler can begin the searches with the leash dragging alongside the dog. The trainer can make the determination as to which set the leash can come off completely. Remember the dog is a little easier to control compared to the High Range Level dog. As the team completes each search, the trainer should always be observing and encouraging the dog team.

Day 1/2

Whether you go right into box searches with the dog by itself or with toy enticement, you can follow the routines that were just described. The toys should only be required for the first two days. However, be prepared to throw the toy for the dog if required for an additional day or two. This is done at the trainer's discretion.

As prescribed in the planning, use seven neutral boxes with all of the HBs for the first two days. It will help the trainer to decide if the dog is comfortable with the training concept and if not, whether or not an additional day or two of using the toy as an enticement, or a continuation of the four HBs with the eight neutral boxes are required. In my opinion it will not be hard to determine. However, if the dog regresses at the start of the second week, then go back to using the boxes or the toy for a short while. All dogs will regress to some degree during training at some point in time. This is part of the learning process. Do not let it concern you, and especially the handler as this can be a real downer if it happens more than once.

Learn to deal with this in a positive manner and always go back to some of the basics and evaluate each time it happens.

Day 3/4

Repeat the first two days, except now (1) let the line drag and (2) the trainer should not entice the dog with the toy. A toy will be in each HB. Once again, if the dog starts to get too far ahead of the handler and starts to miss a box or two, the handler should be instructed to step on the line and voice command the dog not to miss the box. If the dog passes any box, command it back to the missed box for a sniff. This is called nagging and dogs hate to be nagged and eventually will not miss any box at all. Some dogs are worse than others for surging and missing boxes. They are much like humans; looking for the easy way out by taking short-cuts.

During these two days, and at the trainer's discretion, the handler should continue to walk beyond the dog as it sits after each command to SIT is given. As mentioned earlier, start with three paces beyond the dog. Increase the distance only when advised by the trainer.

Days 5 to 8

During these next few days, decrease the number of boxes to be used, use no toys at all for enticement other than to reward the dog from the find. In this case, the handler can present the reward. The line may still have to be used or allowed to drag – use your discretion. Set up a series of four neutral boxes and one HB in this sequence.

Note: Use one explosive group (HB) per set. The dog will find each HB group five times per set. There are four HB groups in all completed five times per set and there are five sets that the dog has to accomplish. HB1 is done first and last.

Set 1:
HB1, B2, B3, B4, B5, then
B1, HB1, B3, B4, B5, then
B1, B2, HB1, B4, B5, then
B1, B2, B3, HB1, B5, then
B1, B2, B3, B4, HB1 – Set #1 finished

For Set 2 replace HB1 with HB2 and repeat the sequence.
For Set 3 replace HB2 with HB3 and repeat the sequence.
For Set 4 replace HB3 with HB4 and repeat the sequence.
For Set 5 replace HB4 with HB1 and repeat the sequence.

Once each dog has completed the 25 Searches, put the HBs away for the rest of the day.

Complete these exercises each day for all four days. During these four days the dog should have adjusted comfortably and remain sitting as the handler continues on to the end of the row. These four days are usually the "Transition Point" for the dog. However, if an extra day is required, do it. As long as the progress is sure and steady, then you are on the right track.

Day 9/10

During these two days, break up all of the explosive groups and place each explosive separately in its own HB. Now there will be approximately six HBs with its own explosive.

Place four neutral boxes and one HB in a row. Use only one HB per search and repeat as often as possible during these two days using any sequence set out by the trainer. All of these searches should be off line and completed at a good and happy tempo. By now the box searches may become more of a bore for the handler than the dog. However, complete these until you are sure the dog is sound.

Days 11 to 18

During these next six to seven days, box training will be combined with empty office areas and office storage areas. If you wish to continue using the row of boxes with an HB in sequence, do so. However, so much time has already been spent on box searches in sequence that at this point it probably would be better to push the dog at this range level to observe where they stand in terms of searching ability and the intensity of the search. What I have done and suggest is to forget the row searching and go into placing the HB of choice in one empty office and a neutral box in each of the other rooms. Complete these as was done for the High Range Level dogs. The dog should be comfortable searching the empty rooms. Complete these as many times as required. The dog should not feel any discomfort searching the empty rooms; now move the searching to the storage areas.

Place a box on each side of the area in whatever sequence desired. Place each box at a different height. Begin your searches left to right. Turn this into an exciting game for the dog, searching low and high for these boxes. As soon as it nears the HB, have the handler step back and observe. This is the same as was done for High Range Level dogs. The trainer will ensure the dog Sits at the right moment and the handler misses nothing. Each day the dog becomes better, remove one of the neutral boxes. Continue to observe each day, removing the second neutral box until only the HB is left. Now your dog is ready for Scenario Training. Remember, as you continue on with the training, keep the tempo constant and lots of praise.

Low Range Level

Dogs categorized in this level offer a trainer his/her greatest challenges. In most instances very little time will be spent on these dogs due to the fact that:

a) they require a great deal of attention, time and an extreme amount of patience; and,

b) there is a lack of expertise on the trainer's part.

However, cut your losses on the low-end dogs. I still take the time to train a dog in this level if the dog is showing me that it has "that something special" in its personality. This is usually indicative of a slow maturing dog. If, as a trainer, you are able to recognize this, do not wash the dog from your program. Take your time with it as these dogs usually make excellent working dogs. Take the time and make the effort to train these dogs. If you can train these dogs, you can train any dog. The initial stages of training for these dogs is very basic and simple; however, this is usually a long-term project.

With dogs of the previous range levels, all of their training progressed in terms of Days 1 to 5, etc. For the dogs at this level, training should be conducted in stages. As with the other dogs beforehand, the following is what I will do to entice the dog to enjoy and want to continue the game.

Stage 1

With this stage I will usually pick the dog's favorite toy and play retrieve with the dog over and over until it gets tired. This should be done outside first because outside retrieval comes naturally for most dogs where there are fewer environmental distractions to bother them.

Handlers usually find the ball is the most commonly used toy. But for Stage 1, find a good size Kong (medium) and a hollowed-out plastic rod. I prefer to introduce these two different toys to the dog(s) at this Stage for a couple of reasons:

a) To introduce a toy that can hold explosives or explosive scented material;

b) To introduce a distraction to the dog(s).

Introducing explosives or explosive scented material and placing it inside the toy is done to associate the toys to the scent of explosives, but in a fun or playful manner. The Kong will have the scented material, i.e., cloth or explosive wrappers, and the hollowed rod will have the actual explosive inside. The Kong can have one or two different scents while the rod will have one or two other scents.

Along with the introduction of explosive scents, via the Kong and rod, you are also creating a distraction for the dog(s). How is this a distraction? Dogs of this range level, due to slow maturity, tend to be somewhat single-minded. What I mean is, if you continually played fetch with a ball, the dog tends to think only BALL and does not want to chase and fetch anything else. It is the lack of maturity that makes its interest in "chasing the prey" and "fetching it back" to the handler appear non-existent and/or weak. The interest appears to be there but it does not have that extreme zeal that is so predominant in the other range levels. Hence, I like to use both the Kong and the rod to build on the fun of the game. The immediate change of the toy creates the distraction by making the dog chase these two toys a little harder, find them, and really sniff or take note of them.

This is where the handler/trainer should really vocalize in a positive way and encourage the dog to fetch them back to the handler. As soon as the dog brings one item back, then throw the other item and so on. What I am doing is looking for an increase in enjoyment level. A stronger desire to chase the toys harder, look for them longer and fetch them back to the handler faster. If I see these characteristics in the dog appearing a little stronger each time the team goes out to play, then I know there is a good chance that this dog, with time, can become a reliable detector dog. In such cases, the handler/trainer should continue with this regimen until the dog greets the handler/trainer every morning with the anticipation of more throwing games. If the dog shows no additional interest during the first two weeks of this first stage, then give the dog to a family to enjoy.

Continue this first stage until you are satisfied with what you are seeing, but do not rush this first step. Remember, be Patient – Patient – Patient!

Stage II

This level is a little more demanding for the dog. I begin this stage by starting with boxes. I set out three to four boxes in an open field area. Inside one box will be the dog's toy. It is placed in the box unknown to the dog. I will then bring the dog to the area and encourage it verbally to find its toy and then let it go on its own. Ultimately the dog should go off on its own if for no other reason than to investigate the boxes. When it finds the box with the toy inside, it will become very surprised and will investigate more thoroughly on its own. At this point of investigation (this happens fast) praise the dog for a job well done. Even while you are praising it, the dog may be pawing at it or trying to stick its head inside to bite at the toy. This is okay. Just keep going to the dog, take the toy out and throw it to play fetch. Continue again with the same exercise. But this time, place the hide box in a different location. This can be done while the dog is away fetching the toy. Now go back to the start position and place the dog in a sit position. Make the dog remain in a sit position while you walk away to place the toy in the hide box. Making the dog remain in a sit position each time you go out to hide the ball helps get the dog used to the SIT command. Commanding the dog to SIT when it locates the toy can affect the dog in a negative way. However, the dog does eventually catch on to the game. However, I do not suggest you command the dog to SIT at each find until the dog is very comfortable with the game. It usually takes three to six tries to get into it comfortably. Also, when the handler/trainer hides the toy in a different location, make sure that the person is pretending to hide the ball in each box. Do not just go to the hide box to place the toy inside. The dog figures out this game very fast and eventually will go directly to the box the handler/trainer placed the toy inside.

Each time the dog gets better at it, increase the number of boxes to be laid out. By the end of the week, the dog should be comfortable with being commanded to SIT at the hide box. When the dog is doing well with the outside environment and its intensity and desire appears to be growing, it is time for the third stage.

Stage III

This is usually the final stage for the dog. We will now bring the boxes inside, laying them out in the same manner as was done outside. This may be a little bit of a distraction for the dog. However, if it is, it will be short lived. If the dog has no problem with working the boxes inside or has worked out its problems, then it is time to place the boxes in a row as you would if you were training a dog of the mid-range level or high-range level. If it appears that your dog is not going to be enticed by searching boxes, then try switching to using a hollowed-out rod. Start by throwing it in whatever direction in the open field for Stage I. For Stage II, throw the rod in such a manner that the dog cannot see where it is thrown. Then have the dog look for it. You have added a degree of difficulty for the dog at this stage by waiting a few minutes before you let the dog go to search. For Stage III, throw the rod inside, on slippery floors, under vehicles, on top of boxes, on small piles of lumber, etc. Once it appears that the dog is comfortable with searching for the rod inside buildings, you are now ready to have the dog search open walls, low and high for its toy (rod).

With these low-range dogs, it is important to remember:

a) be extremely patient;

b) know when to tell yourself the dog is not going to make it;

c) not everyone will be able to help you out with a dog of this range level – not everyone has that experience;

d) be aware of timing for dogs at all the levels;

e) use a system of training that suits the dog – do not stick with one system to find out it doesn't work for the dog. Change it. Don't just wash out the dog because it doesn't meet a system criteria. Find out if another system will capture its interest before you decide to wash out the dog; and

f) make a plan of how you are going to train the dog. It is important to set goals of what you wish to achieve with the dog at all the range levels, how fast you realistically will achieve these goals and which system you wish to use to achieve these goals.

Once you have achieved all of the above, you and the dog are now ready for the multi-explosives hide boxes. Keep in mind the dog's range level. I would suggest that the dog's toy be included in the HB with the explosives. Keep the second toy on your body, so that the dog's saliva will not contaminate the explosives.

I repeat these words again – be patient, take your time and things will go well. Follow the same sequences as you would for the mid-range dog, but do not set a time on the training steps. Complete each step in a manner that is favorable to the dog before going on to the next one. As the dog gets more confidence, more can be achieved.

Once the dog has reached a good level of competency, i.e.:

a) working hard to find the HB;

b) showing good signs of indication and confirmation;

c) not leaving the hide once found; and

d) staying in a sit position for long periods of time.

The team is now ready for the next part – Search Scenario Training.

Scenario Training

Scenario training is comprised of two parts: search theory and search scenario training.

Search Theory

Knowing how to efficiently and effectively search is equally as important as the dog. Search theory is the art of understanding how to search any given area in a specific manner relative to the environmental makeup of the area and to air current patterns.

Search theory teaches us why we should search a specific area in a certain manner, while search scenarios teach us how to search a specific area in an *efficient* and *effective* manner. The operative words here are efficient and effective. Search theory teaches us how air currents, hot or cold environments, extreme temperature changes, the manner in which a dog is worked and search patterns can cause extreme grief or failure in your searches. These are all things that should be addressed in theory first and not during search scenarios. In order to put theory into one smooth package of efficiency and effectiveness, the handler must first understand why it is important to assess the area to be searched before the search begins.

Assessing an area is the act of evaluating its physical contents or makeup. This specific act allows handlers to determine:

● How the area will be searched (search pattern)
● How the dog will be handled
● Observation of air vents on inside searches and air currents on outside searches

- How big an area or how many items to be searched
- Temperature of the search area

A good assessment of the search area or items assists the handler to create a plan in a very short period of time. With practice, the handler will be able to assess the call and have a plan ready to work within a minute or less. The handler will then be able to work the dog in a manner prescribed by plan and search an area or items without having to redo the search, while at the same time taking into account the dog's reaction or indications to the physical makeup of the area or item and possible air movement.

This sounds like a lot and somewhat overwhelming. However, it is very easy to do if properly taught.

Air Currents

Whether you search inside or outside, moving air (vents and open windows and doors) will either disturb the scent cone enough that it will either lead the dog to the source or to miss the source completely. During outside searches, air currents can cause greater problems for the detection team. Outside wind, as opposed to moving inside air, can increase the area to be searched and raise the degree of difficulty for the dog.

In search theory, it should be important to let the handler know that while air bounces off walls, furniture, floors, etc., the dog can, with the handler's help, narrow down the areas to be searched in a short time, or move to another area. Outside searches are usually not confined to an area the size of an office, but can extend to a size in acres. Now the team is searching for the scent cone that may be either on top of the surface or being swirled in the air at great distances. Where does the team start first? Which is the best way for the team to search, off-line or on-line? Should the search begin:

a) into the wind?
b) at right angles to the wind? or
c) with the wind?

Search theory teaches the handler how to deal with these questions. Search theory teaches the handler how the search will be conducted from the assessment of the area and of the wind. As a result, an efficient and effective search can be completed.

High Temperature/Low Temperature Environments

It is important to know that searching in different temperatures can influence the outcome of the search. Searches during temperature extremes can cause the handler to become easily confused by the dog's behavior. For example, a handler/dog team can enter into a room where there is a hide of a quarter pound of TNT in an 8' x 10' room where the temperature is above 85°F (29°C). As the dog enters the room, it begins to wildly circle, searching high and low. The dog becomes frustrated and may even begin to whine. All of a sudden, the dog confirms and sits. The handler is perplexed. The dog didn't appear to find the source, yet it is sitting in confirmation. What search theory will teach the handler is that the higher the temperature, the greater the chance of the room becoming completely saturated with the scent to the point that the room becomes the source to the dog. This is because heat causes the molecular build-up of the scent cone to expand and bounce off of one another to the point where the room will become saturated, causing the frustration of the dog and confusion of the handler. In this case, the handler has a choice. Firstly, he/she can confirm to the bomb-tech that there is an explosive in the room, or secondly, he/she can in some manner slow down the molecular activity by cooling down the room or aerating it to the point where the dog can concentrate on searching the physical aspects of the room (desks, garbage cans, etc.). The dog will go to the source – this does happen.

On the other side of the coin, the handler/dog team now has to search the same room where the temperature is below 0°F (-17°C). The handler/dog team has to search for the same amount of explosive (quarter pound of TNT). After the handler assesses the situation, the team enters to search. A slight indication, but nothing found – no confirmation. This now becomes a downer for the handler. There is a hide but it cannot be found. Once again, the handler has two choices. Firstly, the handler can leave the area – nothing found, or secondly, the room can be re-searched. I would take the second choice. Why? Although the dog did not confirm, there was a slight moment of interest for the dog and the area is quite cold. This would be one of the very few times I would re-search the room. However, I would pay particular attention to the area of interest to the dog and do a more in-depth search with the dog.

What I have learned is that searching in colder temperatures creates some very distinct problems. The reaction of the dog is the extreme opposite to that of the dog doing the search in the room when the temperature was very warm. The colder the temperature, then the closer the scent cone stays to the source. There virtually can be no scent cone at all.

For the best results in cold temperature searches, the search pattern of the dog should be more concentrated or tighter. Search everything – front, back, up, down and sideways. However, there is a point in time when searching in temperatures below a certain degree will be fruitless. This, however, should be left to the handler's discretion. He/she knows the capabilities of the dog best.

Extreme Temperature Changes

This is an aspect of the environment that can have or create drastic consequences. Where this is a concern is in areas with cold winters. Extreme temperature changes can cause the scent cone to be sucked away from the dog's nose. In this case, the extreme temperature changes occur from inside to outside. Let me explain.

In search theory, handlers will learn that when extreme hot air meets with extreme cold air, a violent wind stream is created. If the temperature outside of a room or area is -20°F (-28°C) and the temperature inside the room is above 75°F (23°C), there will be violent air currents or winds when a door is opened and the two extremes meet. What you have is a gust of wind created as the cold air rushes in underneath the warm air and the warm air is pushed outside, hence a wind current.

However, as the warm air is rushing out, it is taking with it the scent cone. Now you can see where this can become a serious problem for the handler. This is a generic problem for dog teams stationed in air terminals located in northern climates, or where pallets of cargo (boxes, etc.) are positioned along a wall next to an outside door that has even a quarter to half an inch of space between the door and the floor. There can be as much as five to ten pounds of explosives hidden on the pallet, but if it is situated close enough to the door, the dog could miss the hide completely. In these situations, the handler has the choice of first, making sure the cargo doors remain closed until the search is completed, or second, waiting until the wind currents settle down before the search is resumed. In the case of the cargo situated on the pallets next to the door, only one possible solution exists. Have the dog search between the door and the pallet of boxes. The dog will be guaranteed to get the scent cone.

How the dog is worked – off-line/on-line: this is a bone of contention for many trainers and departments. Which is the best system? I will leave that up to you. I was taught both systems and personally, I found off-line searching to be the most efficient and effective way to search. Remember, the first step to searching was to assess the situation and area to be searched first. In addition to this first step, I found that I could also assess the search the dog was doing better if I was standing back or walking behind the dog as it searched on its own. I could not assess the dog's search if it was on-line.

This is what I call "having sight of the total picture." This allows the handler to assess the dog's progression in a systematic fashion.

1. What has it searched?
2. What has it not searched?
3. What is left to search?
4. Were there any indications from the dog that create suspicions in the handler's mind?

If the dog misses anything, the handler can redirect the dog at any given moment. If the dog expressed any indications, then the handler has the opportunity to redirect the dog to those areas at any given moment to be completely satisfied. Any areas that are searched well are an indication to the handler that these areas need not be searched again. This is the efficiency of a search.

However, I would never refrain from searching on-line. For example, new dogs need to begin on-line. Some dogs can only be worked on-line and there are times when danger to the dog is apparent. I do prefer off-line work, but on-line work serves its purpose as well.

Search Scenario Training

Whereas search theory is learning why we do what we do, search scenario training is learning how to accomplish efficient and effective searches as per the search theory.

It is extremely gratifying to watch green detector dog handlers begin their searches with a mental plan in mind and try to meet problems head on with quick thinking remedies during the search.

For the first week of search scenario training, all hides should be known hides. This is so each handler can begin to understand his/her dog's body language when it enters into the scent cone, when it is indicating the source, when it confirms or when it is indicating anything other than explosives, through observation. This is extremely important for the handler during the first weeks. This beginner imprinting creates very competent and confident handlers who begin to believe in their dogs' abilities as time goes on.

In search scenario training, each area dictates its own search method. There is also a learning format that indicates what should be taught first, because each area builds on the other. The path from easy to a high degree of difficulty is followed with great success.

1. Buildings (inside)
   a) Walls
   b) Rooms
   c) Large work areas, i.e., garages, office workstations
   d) Locker rooms
   e) Motels
2. Vehicles
   a) Buses (inside and outside)
   b) Cars (outside only) and trucks
   c) Heavy equipment
3. Air Terminals
   a) Lobbies (passenger areas)
   b) Cargo (freight)
   c) Baggage
   O floor
   O baggage conveyor belt

4. Aircraft
   a) Inside
   b) Cargo holds
   c) Landing gear receptacles
5. Buried

1. Buildings

This is where search scenario training begins. As a trainer, you should have sites selected a week in advance. If your unit is part of a police service that takes care of a large urban area, you should be able to find several sites to suit training for each night or be able to find a building large enough to offer different areas for every night of the week training is carried out. However, if you are part of a small rural area and do not have the luxury of large buildings or a lot of buildings, then I would suggest that you try to team up with a larger department doing the same training. Otherwise, your program will be frustrated by the lack of training areas.

In Calgary I was always fortunate to have large businesses that would allow us to use their buildings for after-hours training. As well, the Calgary Transit System was always gracious enough to let us use the bus barns for training. The barns were used quite frequently. It is always to the unit's benefit to keep up good relations with other city departments. These people will usually go out of their way to assist you with finding good training sites. Other good training venues are the large professional sports complexes. Good relations with different organizations can be crucial to the success of your training program.

Once you have your site(s) chosen, break your training into these different areas, starting with (1) walls, (2) rooms – big and small, (3) large work areas – work shops, mechanical bay areas, (4) offices and office workstations. The degree of difficulty increases at each area in a progressive and steady manner. This allows the handlers to build on their skills in a consistent fashion. This system also gives the trainer time to adjust the training aspects while they are in progress because it is easier to observe each team work and see problems begin to bud. Let's begin the steps.

a) Walls

For the purposes of this book, let's say the building you have acquired is a large bus barn. You should have already surveyed the areas to be used for beginning scenarios. To begin, select several long and busy walls – walls with extruding pipe works, cupboards, firehose stations, storage bins and lockers. Choose an explosive of the day. All dog teams get the same explosive for the duration of the training session (day or night). Divide the wall into sections, keeping in mind that each section will have a portion of the chosen explosive hidden on it. For each section, alternate low and high hides and vary the amounts of explosive used for each hide. As per the Search Training Rules (Chapter 5), write in your notebook the usual appropriate information (explosive used, quantity, hide location, etc.). On the other walls, have your trainees do similar hides in the same fashion. Instruct them to place the appropriate information within their notebooks as well. Try to have a wall for each dog.

This next step may appear redundant, but I feel it is still very important to continue its use for the first week. At the beginning of each training session, have the trainees search a row of hide boxes. During the first week of Search Scenario Training, I use a different single explosive for each day of the first week of training. I would do something like:

Mondays – TNT and Nitro Base

Tuesdays – RDX

Wednesdays – Slurries/Amm.Nit. Base

Thursdays – PETN & Perchlorates

Fridays – Powders (smokeless and black)

Each day starts with box searches and a new explosive. What this does is program the dog to recognize the scent along the walls as the same scent that came from the box.

After a box search is done by the first handler/team, have the same team approach the wall. However, before the team starts, have the handler assess the wall to create a mental plan. Then have the handler tell you how they will approach the wall for their search. When you are satisfied with their approach to the search, then have them proceed. If you are not satisfied with their approach, then ask specific questions that will make the handler rethink his/her assessment. Once the handler has answered your questions satisfactorily and has given an amended version to the first assessment, have them begin.

Have the team perform low then high search patterns. This allows the dog to work into the scent cone. The first week or two can be known hide searches. For known hides the trainer will, in a loud voice, tell the team they are approaching a hide and tell the handlers to pay close attention to the changes in their dog's behavior. As soon as the dog indicates the source and confirms by sitting, the handler can reward the dog. Lots of praise should be coming from the trainer at this point.

During these low and high search patterns, the dog should be either on-leash, with the leash in the left hand of the handler, or the leash should be dragging under the dog. With leash in left hand or dragging, the handler should (with the right hand) direct the dog to search a specific low area first by tapping lightly with the ends of the fingers and commanding the dog to SEEK or FIND IT. As soon as the dog places its nose on the area to sniff, the handler should be taking a step or two back, ready to tap the next high spot to be searched. This is done as soon as the dog takes its nose away from the first spot. This should be done in an easy, consistently flowing manner – not too slow and not too fast. If the handler is in control of the leash, make sure it is very loose or sagging. If the handler keeps a short, tight leash, it will only provoke the dog to follow and not properly check those areas it was directed to. This is why I prefer the line off, or at the very least dragging.

Begin the same routine with the other handler/dog teams, but with a slight difference. After the second team finishes their wall, have them search the areas that the previous team searched. Continue with these repetitions for each team thereafter.

By the end of the week, each team should have good low/high search patterns and the dogs should be more than competent with indicating and confirming each explosive. As time progresses, continue to use the walls for training.

b) Rooms

This next section flows right along from the wall searches. Why? Because rooms usually have four walls and a door.

Inside are desks, workstations, coffee machines, etc. However, no matter which way you look at a room, the walls are searched first. That is why the segment on walls was done first – to create a flowing search pattern and to learn to recognize the individual explosives. Learning is repetition.

There are some general rules I like handler/dog teams to follow. The reason is to create good work habits and search techniques. In other words, efficiency and effectiveness which equals productive searches and safe searches.

Because "booby-traps" are a reality of biker houses and drug houses, I have a very strict rule about assessing each call. If, during the handler's assessment, the handler notes a door is closed, then there is only one thing the handler/dog team can do. Anytime there is a closed door, no one other than a Bomb Tech (at a real situation) should open that door. However, the handler/dog team can search that door first in a systematic fashion. The dog can sniff the area between the door and the floor first. This should help determine if (1) large amounts of explosives are in the room; and/or (2) if the hide is very close to the door, which would indicate a "booby-trap." Either way, the dog should indicate and confirm.

If nothing is found by the dog at the door, then continue up the left side and right side of the door, as well as the keyhole and doorknob. It is very easy to place a Det-cord around the door to create a "booby-trap." The doorknob, if closed by the bomber, may have explosive residue left on it. Here again, the dog should indicate and confirm. All/any of these confirmations sing of trouble. As a trainer, make sure each door remains closed and have the handler give you his assessment. As per training routine, if the dog does not indicate and confirm at the door, then have the team ready to search. If the dog confirms the presence of an explosive at the door, ask the handler what he/she would do next. The answer should be nothing other than "Call in the Bomb-Tech."

These are little things that you can prepare ahead of time for training. It makes the handler/dog teams think first.

Next, the trainer opens the door for the handler. The room is dark or semi-dark and the handler makes his assessment. If the handler attempts to turn on a light switch, correct this immediately. NEVER TURN LIGHT SWITCHES ON. Remember that you all want to go home in one piece at the end of the

Be aware of new surroundings. It is always safer to be suspicious of unfamiliar things. If it raises a question in your mind, then check it.

shift! As a trainer, suggest the handler use his/her flashlight. Assessment: Have the handler look for the obvious first, for example, pieces of wire on the floor, trip wire, lump under the carpet, anything that may indicate something is out of the norm. When the handler gives you a proper assessment as per your scenario, the handler is ready to search. For the purposes of training, the trainer can put the light switch on.

Searching rooms is relatively simple. However, some rooms are so full of equipment and desks or piles of boxes in the centre or along the walls of the rooms, etc., that areas can be missed. So keep in mind that no handler/dog team should just go in and do a "helter-skelter" search. Each venue, be it an aircraft, vehicle or room, should have its own search plan. I learned a lot of these methods from the Royal Canadian Mounted Police explosives dog handlers. They have been in the business for a long time and I really respect any information they may have with regard to searches.

The one thing I teach in searching is consistency – beginning with the cursory search. A cursory search is a brief, free-roaming search by the dog into any given area. It is a five- to ten-second search with the only goal of trying to locate a hide in a short period. This system helps to save the dog's energy. It is also a safety factor for the handler.

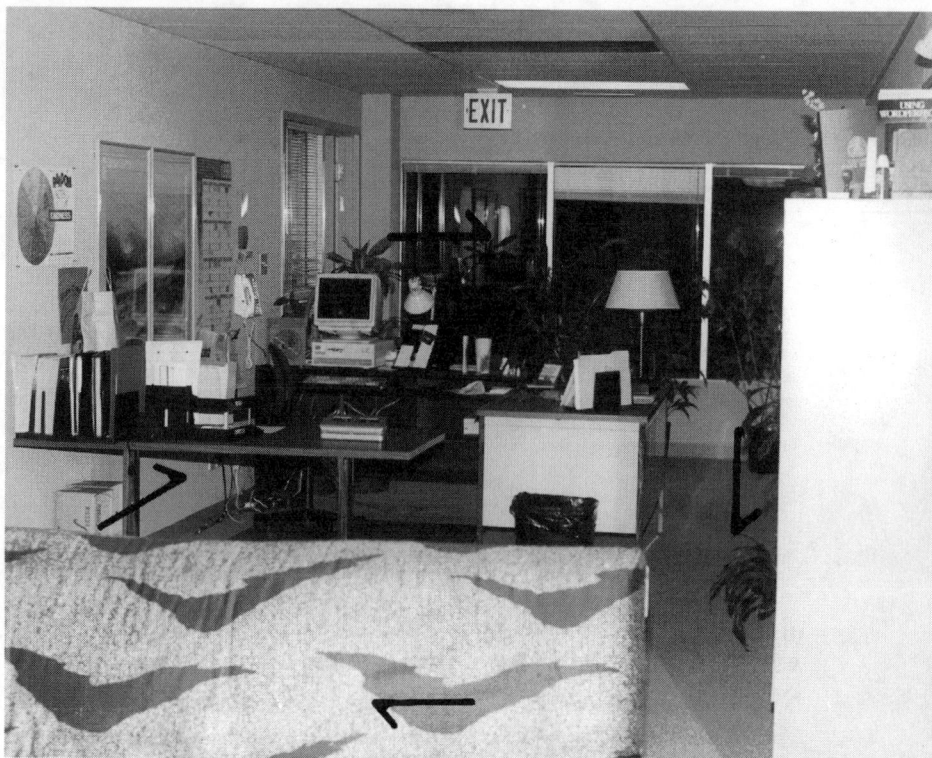

If a large find is discovered (half pound or more), the Bomb-Techs can now come in to render that situation safe. A handler should always keep in mind the path the dog followed to the source. However, if no hide is found, then the next plan of action is followed.

Rooms should be searched left to right or right to left, or begin your search in the direction of your weak side. Since I am right handed, I begin my room searches from left to right. I never venture away from this plan of action unless it is necessary to do so. This search pattern should remain constant. Why? It becomes a safety routine and, should I have to search on-line, going left to right allows me to comfortably direct my dog low and high, because my weak side is where my dog heels.

The handler/dog team now searches the room, left to right, with the handler ahead of the dog (for now). As time progresses, the handler will follow the dog. The handler/dog team searches in a low/high pattern, always remembering that the handler never commands the dog to the next spot while it is still using its nose. It should be commanded just as it finishes or ends searching that particular spot. In time, and with a lot of practice, this will become smooth.

Continue the search. If the dog misses an area or spot, but is still in a search mode, do not worry about that particular location. The dog and handler with time and practice will miss fewer and fewer spots. It is better at this stage to continue with a good search pattern and consistent flow. However, you will have to come back to search that spot at some time during the search of the room. Memory recall is ever so important. It is more important for a handler to remember what has <u>not</u> been searched rather than what has already been searched. As the trainer, you should keep mental notes of what was not searched. With this in mind, ask the handler (when finished searching) to tell you what has not been searched. This is part of every course I have taught and it is very valuable. Handlers will remember everything that was not searched and will take their dog back to those locations automatically once the end of the room is reached. They all pick this up in a matter of days. This becomes ever so apparent when the handler follows the dog on searches. This is efficiency.

Now if the dog is starting to indicate ever so slightly and the handler has not made the connection, you should be telling your trainee to watch his/her dog. Remember, it takes time to understand what is observed and these handlers may not have the expertise that you may have. Just shout it out – "Watch your dog." Being a good trainer is part of the equation.

As the trainer, prepare your rooms with a hide in each room. Be careful at the beginning that you only do one hide per room. If there is more than one hide per room, confusion for the dog and the handler may occur. As with the wall searches, let the handler know when the dog is nearing the hide so he/she can observe the changes in the dog as it enters the scent cone. As a trainer, I believe in helping a new handler as much as possible. I adamantly oppose the type of instruction or training that requires the handler to make the right choices by guessing. All this type of training ever produces is a confused and unconfident handler.

Have each trainee do at least one unknown hide. When each handler is finished with their unknown hide, they can then search the rooms that were completed by the other handlers.

This will at least ensure that each handler/dog team gets more than one or two searches and hides each training session.

c) Large Work Areas

Large work areas are mechanical bay areas, such as those found at transit barns, big trucking companies, etc. These areas usually have large open centres where the vehicles are parked. But along the walls are congested workbenches, tie racks, lockers, etc. These areas usually have small storage rooms along the walls too. Also present is a huge number of scent contaminants, such as oil, diesel, gasoline, cleaning supplies, dust and exhaust fumes. These are excellent for training.

Trainers should section each search area off wall to wall or from a wall to a piece of equipment. These areas should be have lots of area for the handler/dog team to cover and a lot of items to search. This area should have one hide. In these areas, the degree of difficulty should be increased gradually. Have each handler assess the area to be searched. Searching begins with a quick cursory search, five to ten seconds long. If nothing is found (it is not necessary that a source be found on every cursory search), then the handler/dog team begins a systematic low/high search, left to right always. Be sure the handlers are made aware of possible air currents as these areas usually have large circulating air units running at all times. These can direct scent or take it away.

As the handler/dog team nears a hide, again, let them know about it. Each time a handler finishes an area, have them tell you what changes they observed in their dog that told them the dog was in the scent cone. When you feel the handlers are beginning to comprehend indications/confirmation, then you can slowly refrain from telling them when they are near the scent cone. But always be ready to help out should a problem occur. This way of training, where each handler is assisted, really speeds up the process.

Have all the handler/dog teams search each other's areas. Once again, have the handlers do hides as well. A properly planned out search area will assist each and every handler in becoming capable in assessing search areas for training, setting out hides and observing each other's dog's character- istics. This is important for critiquing each other's work.

d) Locker Rooms

Lockers add another dimension to the task of searching. Some lockers are built into walls, others are along walls. Some lockers are made of wood, while others are made of metal. Some are tall, others are short and some are deep and others are shallow. What lockers have in common is the inconsistency of where the scent can travel. In most cases, the handler/dog teams search low/high along the fronts of the lockers and this may be the only way they can be searched if they are built into the wall.

Some handler/dog teams have difficulty with lockers. The biggest problem is that the fronts are usually shiny and hard, which makes it hard for the dog to grasp with its nails. This causes the dogs to slip around and frustrates them into not searching. This usually, in time, frustrates the handlers to the limit. Emotions begin to run high, which dogs usually pick up, and no-win situation is created.

Solution: Although I haven't used it myself, rubber dog booties sprayed with stick-em were placed on the dog's front paws. I was told it worked. Another solution is to just practice.

Another reason for difficulty is that the scent is usually drawn out the back of the locker through the small holes or joints, thereby making it very difficult for the dog to indicate or confirm the source.

Solution: While performing the low/high search patterns, and the dog is just finishing a low search, get the dog up on its hind legs to investigate the bottom corners of the lockers, half-way up the joints on both sides and the handle (if lockers are two-tiered) or the joints along both sides and the handles of tall lockers. If a system such as this can be created, they should be able to get some kind of indication. Another solution, and only if the lockers are stacked against the wall, is to search low/high between the wall and the lockers and at both ends. As I stated earlier, the scent is sometimes drawn out the back of the lockers and then down the wall along the floor towards either ends of the lockers. Whatever way you look at this, lockers are not as easy as they may seem.

As a trainer, experiment with different amounts of explosives in lockers. When setting up training scenarios for trainees, try to give each handler his/her own bank of lockers, after which they can search each other's. The more practice, the better the teams become.

e) Motels

Previously slept-in motel rooms are an excellent venue to search. You have the recent body odor of one or more people. There usually is food, alcohol, cigarette butts and toiletries – many, many different air contaminating scents. Although usually small, these rooms can be booked ahead of time. If you are going to practice in this setting, have the motel staff set aside five to six rooms, which can be on different floors. Have only two of the rooms with a hide in each one. Ensure that the handler/dog teams have to search two or three empty rooms first before they find the first hide. This will help build up stamina in the dog. Use garbage-filled waste containers, mattresses, counters, or drawers to hide explosives. Remember the rules of search training.

In the case of motels, the handler/dog teams should be well advanced by this time. Therefore, this is the best venue to do totally unknown hides for all the trainees. As each handler/dog team finishes, they can then observe the next handler do their searches. Each handler still should do an assessment, so don't be afraid to set out some wire, or a battery on the floor just to see how aware each handler is. Also remember, the assessment is always done from the doorway.

2. Vehicles

Any kind of vehicle (heavy-duty equipment, cars, light and heavy trucks, or buses) is difficult to do. But there are ways of making the search easier for the dog. Any vehicle has its weak areas. This is especially true of vehicles, especially older ones. They rust, they twist, they separate at the seams and they wear down. Newer vehicles, on the other hand, make it harder to detect scent, because they are more airtight due to far less wear and tear. Nonetheless, it is not impossible to detect scent. One way of seeing just how airtight a newer vehicle is compared to an older one is to turn the ignition to air conditioning, put the heater on and fan on high and close all the doors. Wait a few moments, then move the back of your hand along all of the door cracks and along the trunk. I would also tell you to try this along the fire-wall and under the trunk, but it is impossible to place your hands there. On new vehicles, the air coming through these points is very faint, but there is enough coming through for a dog to detect an explosive. However, as you run the back of your hand along the same areas of an older car, the differences are like night and day. The air coming through the various areas is coming through quite strongly. If you do this test, make a mental note of exactly where the air was escaping. These are generic areas where the dogs can investigate. The points of escaping air are pretty much the same on all cars with a few exceptions. Light and heavy duty trucks are much the same way.

a) Buses (inside and outside)

Buses are fairly easy. City Transit buses can be used by the end of the second week, especially if they exist in the same building being used for wall searches. Begin the search training on the outside first. The reason for this is that searching the outside (with a few exceptions) of the bus is almost the same as searching the walls. There are many places to hide small amounts of explosives and the outside of the bus still allows the low/high search pattern. However, an added feature is that explosives can also be placed in the motor compartment and in the wheel wells. This is Step One in graduating to vehicles. Searching inside simulates searching in an aircraft because most newer passenger buses have similar seats and overhead compartments, only smaller than the aircraft. You can see why I make a connection between buses and aircraft. You can also see the connection of how training at one venue prepares the team for the next venue.

The best time to use transit buses for training is after work hours. This guarantees there will be an abundance of buses to practice on. Begin with outside searches on the buses first. Most of the buses will be parked end-to-end, so this will allow the trainer to give at least three to four buses (parked end-to-end) to each handler/dog team to search. For the outside searches, low/high, you only need to use one quarter to half pound pieces of explosive. However, if you choose to hide the explosives in the engine compartment or on top of the fuel tank (use these areas only if you are entering the third week of training), then use explosives that weigh half a pound or more.

Place the explosives in spots that you would want the dog to investigate on its own, i.e., on top of the tires, in the wheel wells, in the engine compartments, etc. Dogs have great memory recall and will investigate these areas over and over again with very little encouragement. Enter the number of each bus (with a hide) in your notebook. If your trainees are setting out hides, make sure they do the same.

Begin searches right to left; this is the opposite to inside searches. (Once again, if you have to search online, your dog will heel on your weak side – in my case, on my left – leaving your strong hand free to direct the dog.) By this time the dog should be searching off-line (or line dragging), but following the handler. Should a dog try to get by, just press its head into the bus as it tries to go between the bus and the handler's leg and soon it will stop surging. In time, the dog will search the buses and other vehicles on its own while the handler stands back and observes what is not investigated by the dog. Always keep an eye on the dog for the handler in case something is missed. Remember, for new handlers this can be taxing because they are not yet thinking in an orderly fashion.

For inside searches, use a half-pound or more of explosives. In the beginning, use one bus for two hides. One hide at the front driver's area and one at the back area. Have each handler/dog team search a bus each. The same buses that were used for the outside searches can be used for the inside searches, as long as the explosives used for the outside searches have been removed. This will prevent confusion for the handler and the dog in case the dog gets a whiff of scent coming from outside. But if you can use different buses, it would be better. Be sure the door to the bus is closed before the search begins.

Using two inside hides per bus (one front and one back) helps the handler/dog team create good and safe work habits. It teaches the handlers to get their dogs to investigate the doors for scent before opening them. As it is not necessary to assess the search at this stage, it perhaps is more important to see if there is an explosive close by the door. Why? The reason for this is if the handler opened the door immediately and went inside to assess, then called the dog to come inside, the dog might go by the first hide. Having the handler investigate the doorway before entering will alert the dog that an explosive is nearby (pooled scent). Therefore, as it enters the bus up the steps, it will stay up front and investigate the scent to its source instead of running straight up the steps and to the back. You are now teaching this team to check the front of the bus first or become systematic. Having a hide at the rear teaches the dog to go to the back of the bus thereafter (cursory). It also shows the handler the quick changes in the dog's personality when it is searching, indicating, then confirming.

After a few of these bus hides have been completed, the trainer can use one explosive hide per every three to four buses, i.e., each handler/dog team will now have to search two to three buses before the hide is found. The hide can be placed front, back or mid-way on the bus, either at floor level or just above the floor at seat level. Each time the handler/dog teams go through the "check the door rituals," the handler can send the dog on a cursory search from the opened door. Now, for the first time, you will see the dog check the front first then go straight back but casually checking both the left and right sides and jumping on the seats. As soon as it hits the scent cone, it will stop to investigate. Now the handler, at this time, can come closer and encourage the dog to FIND IT until the source is found and the dog confirms. The handler has saved the team a lot of work. Once the explosive is removed, the team can now finish the rest of the bus. This stage should also teach the dogs to become more comfortable searching between the seats (getting ready for aircraft).

After this is completed with success and the teams are looking confident, the buses will be used for one more step. It is this step that particularly pertains to aircraft searches. Inside the bus, just below the ceiling, are large plastic advertising signs. These are going to simulate overhead baggage bins that are found in aircraft and travel buses. Place the hides behind these signs, one per bus. Make sure these hides are at least a half-pound piece. The first hides should be situated at the mid-way part of the bus, on either side. This will allow the dog to run into the scent cone and investigate. After the handler does the assessment, the dog can be sent on a cursory search. As soon as the dog gets wind of the scent cone, the handler can begin to encourage the dog to SEEK or FIND IT. Because the scent cone will be so big at this point in time, the dog will most likely be lifting its head and jumping from seat to seat on either side. Now is when the handler takes control of the dog's energy and frustration and does a systematic search.

Start the team about four seats away from the source. Have the dog check under the seat first, then on top of the seat, and then on its hind legs to investigate the signs. Now do the same system to the seating area across the aisle. First check the floor area, then on top of the seat to check seat level and finally on its hind legs to check the signs above. However, if the dog doesn't want to leave the area, then work it. What this means is that the dog has found the source close by. Repeat this back to the other side and do the system all over again. Then they should go back down to the other side following the same system until the dog comes into the scent cone area. At this time, it should go up on its hind legs to investigate the source, then sit. However, if it is close, but not close enough and is reaching over top of the next seat up, then encourage the dog to get over to that seat to confirm and sit.

Now the dog and handler have a figure eight, low/high search pattern that will be used for aircraft. With something so simple to search as the bus, the team has used it to beyond its normal potential.

b) Cars/Trucks

Automobiles are definitely the toughest venue to search. Unless we are looking for drugs, the insides of vehicles need not be searched with a dog for reasons of safety. The inside work is always left to the expertise of the Bomb Techs. We do not want to be searching an area and have the dogs crawling over the top of seats, especially if someone may have placed a pressure switch right under a seat.

Vehicles are searched with a system too, right to left with the dog following the handler's commands and moves. Under normal conditions, I instruct handlers not to allow their dogs to jump up or place their paws on the vehicles for obvious reasons of safety. However, we sometimes are not afforded that luxury because some detection dogs (EDDs) are small in stature (Labs, Spaniels, etc.) and they most likely will have to place their paws on a vehicle to reach the scent cone. I have also seen larger dogs have to lift themselves onto the fender of a car or higher up along a window crack to investigate the scent because these are the only places the scent is coming out. This can happen if the wind is swirling under the vehicle and around it, if the search is being done out of doors. Normally, most dogs can reach high enough with their noses while standing on the ground and that is all that is required.

As was done on the outside bus searches, the dogs on their own should be sticking their heads into wheel wells, into the grill, under bumpers and under the car. If they are not placing their heads into these areas then we have to get them to do this by giving them a reason to do so. These are the same places that we will begin the hides.

For first time training on vehicles for new teams, I have found it best to teach the dogs and handlers in a step by step fashion. I usually start with an explosive that is either TNT BASED or NG BASED. These two explosives have the strongest odors and are therefore easier for the dog to find or follow a scent cone. As a result, we teach the dog in a quicker fashion and with greater success.

Select a row of vehicles (about five vehicles/cars or trucks). Pick two of them to be used for the hides. On one vehicle place a hide of half a pound or more on top of the rear axle under the car. It can be placed next to either a rear tire or near the middle. On another vehicle place the other hide on top of the motor next to the firewall. Take special care that the two hide vehicles are not so close that their scent cones will be interfering with one another, causing the dog some confusion. Close hides or hides within the same proximity can be done later on in the course or specifically after the course when the dogs are more confident and accurate.

Hides that are placed under the vehicle somewhere or on top of the motor under the hood are classified as outside hides. For the majority of venues there should be a soak time of no less than 30 minutes. Soak time is the minimum time permitted to allow the scent of the explosive to escape into the air to create a scent cone before the dog is allowed to begin its search. However, for vehicles, aircraft and packages/luggage there should be a minimum of 60 minutes soak time.

While doing the outside searches on the vehicles, it is still important to try to get the dogs to search or investigate the cracks or joints of the doors and the trunk, which on a vehicle would be considered an inside search. Do this even though

Explosives are most likely to be found around the motor or inside the passenger area of a vehicle. Explosives located on top of the engine, for example, can be detected by the dog from a number of locations (see the next four photos). Confusion arises when the handler thinks the dog should confirm at the engine.

there are no explosives placed inside of the vehicle. This is so the dogs get used to searching the areas indicated by the handler's commands and motions.

Because of what we are trying to accomplish at this time, the cursory search is not important. It is more important to keep the dog and the handler focused on completing successful low/high search patterns on the car and as a result the

The scent will fall along the engine block on either side or at the back onto the transmission or along the top of the engine towards the grill (see next photo). This is why it is critical that the team understand how air currents can affect the search.

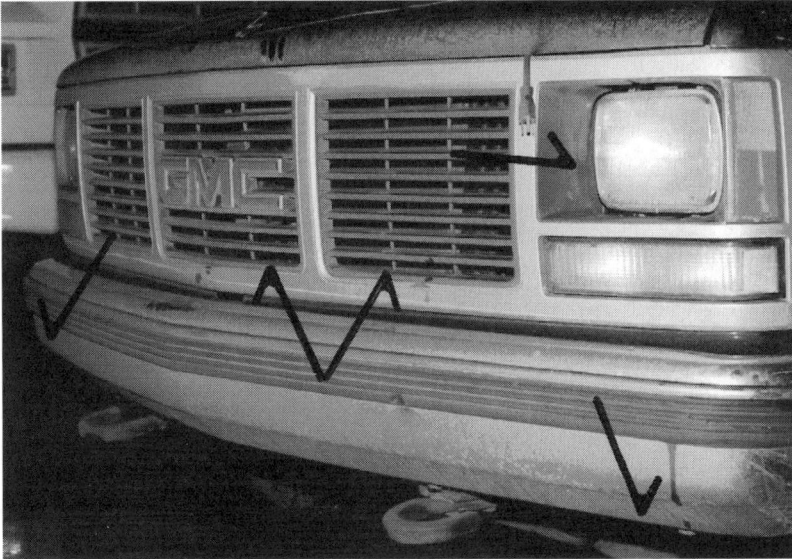

Scent will come out of many places along the grill of the vehicle. Always check the grill, turnlights, headlights, on top of the bumper and under the bumper.

dog gets to find a hide by placing its nose into specific areas as directed by its handler. Have the handler/dog team get accustomed to searching all aspects of the vehicles first. The team can start at any position on the car, searching in a right to left direction around the vehicle and into the wind if this is an out of doors scenario. If this is an indoor search, make your trainees aware of circulating air fans and air ducts.

Wheel wells are a very important and easy location to check for explosives hidden on the engine and sometimes hidden inside of the vehicle. It depends how old the vehicle is and how many holes are in the floor or firewall.

The scent from an explosive on the engine can find its way to the underside of the vehicle, or to the inside. It may surprise the handler if the dog confirms at one of the door joints. Again, it depends on the age of the vehicle.

Because the dogs may not be used to searching vehicles, an on-line search may be required for the first set of cars until the dogs realize that this is all part of the fun. This should always be at the trainer's discretion. Even though a handler may not want to do the search on-line, you should remind the handler that this is to prevent any problems that may cause the dog to regress and that it is only for a short time, but nonetheless it is very important to do at this moment.

Get the dog to check all wheel wells, left and right sides of the tire, as well as on top. Have the dogs check underneath the car along the bottom of the rocker panels and frame. As soon as the dog checks under and is pulling its nose away from under the frame, then direct the dog to search along the bottom door joint then up higher along the door joint as far as its nose will reach without it jumping on the car to get higher, then back down to the underside of the car. When the dog is reaching at its highest point with its nose, the handler should then be taking one or two steps along, ready to direct the dog to the next low area. This is done in a smooth flowing fashion all around the whole vehicle. Continue along under bumpers and into the grills. Once the dog has found the cone of scent, have the handler drop the line as soon as the dog begins to react to it or shows signs of interest. The handler can take a step back and, without any immediate encouragement, let the dog work it out on its own. If the source of the scent is coming from under the car the dog will in most cases crawl right under to the source and just remain there in a down or prone position. For now it is okay, as long as it is not touching the source. What I do to start fixing this, is call the dog out and then redirect it to that same spot it went in. As soon as the dog puts its nose back to get another sniff at it there will probably be a race between the handler and the dog whether the command to sit is given or the dog sits before the command is given. In all, this is usually a very positive event for both dog and handler.

If the dog continues to do this and some dogs do, do not get discouraged. It is not such a bad and notorious thing that the dog should remain prone under the vehicle at the source. Just keep working on it. Another way to try and correct this action is to have the trainer tell the handler he/she is close and to watch for the usual signs, or for the handler to do his/her known hides and to watch for the usual signs. Instead of letting the dog crawl under the vehicle all of the way, command the dog to sit each time the dog gets its head just under the frame or bumper. Eventually the dog will learn to anticipate that the handler will be doing something every time it goes under the vehicle and will confirm in a proper sitting fashion. It all takes time and patience.

Another interesting thing that I have witnessed a majority of EDDs do on the older model or well miled-out vehicles is to give a lot of attention to the underside of the engine where the oil filter is located. In each of the cases, the area around the filter was thickly coated with old burned oil and dirt. Most dogs would go under to investigate. Some would spend considerable time at the filter, back out and then remain standing and looking over at the handler as if it were confused and not sure if it should remain and or sit to confirm. Others would stick their heads under the vehicle at that location, back out and continue to the front of the vehicle, stick their heads as far under as they dared, come back out and go back to the first location and then leave to continue on with the search. It always confuses the handlers into thinking that there is something there and they have the strongest urge to command their dogs to sit. It has always baffled me. This was what my first EDD (Arco) would do. What Arco taught me to do with him and other dogs I have trained was to just let them do their investigation and to keep my mouth shut (no encouragement). As soon as he would come back out to look at me I would just ignore his stature and re-command him to FIND IT. I did not want to create a problem when I didn't understand what he was doing. I also have to thank my trainer at the time, Brian Amm, for making me practice this over and over again. Brian had no clues either at that time. We both surmised and concluded, without proof however, that there were probably similarities of odors or scents between the burned oil combined with the dirt and a German explosive called DM-12 (PETN mixed with coal oil or kerosene). In any event the course of action that I was taught I still use today with very good results.

As soon as the dogs understand the concept of investigating the grill, wheel wells, under rocker panels and bumpers, it is now time to introduce them to inside hides. These are the hides placed inside of the passenger compartments and trunk. The dog is still going to be searching the undersides too but this time, while it is searching high (door joints and trunk joints), it is going find something there. Getting the dog to investigate these areas thoroughly takes a lot of work on the dog's part. Remember, to help the dogs understand how to search on vehicles and to know what they are searching for requires the handlers to direct the dogs to the right locations and for the trainer to allow the hides to soak long enough.

Give the dogs a reason to investigate a specific area, i.e., doors and trunks. Show that if they do investigate (sniff) these areas they will find something and get their reward. There are two approaches to this. One is to have a large enough amount of explosive placed inside of the trunk area or on the floor of the vehicle's interior. Then let the hides soak for a long period of time (one hour or more). Then have the handler/dog teams do the searches. The second method, which is the one I prefer to use, is to take little pieces of explosive about half the size of your baby finger or the paper wrappers, place them inside of the door jambs or trunk lid frames and close them on the explosives. These pieces can be placed along the bottom of the door and up the sides. Vary the positions so that the dogs have a good variance of positions to cover. The soak times for these hides need only be 30 minutes (if they soak longer it is not a problem).

Explosives located inside the passenger area (under the front drivers seat, for example) can cause the dog to confirm almost anywhere, from the back or trunk area, the cracks on the door, the front wheel wells or under the vehicle from either side.

Pick out five cars to do this on, making sure that all door hides or the large inside hides are hidden on opposite sides if the vehicles are parked side by side and close together. For trunk hides, place them in every other vehicle. This will prevent the dogs from becoming mixed-up or frustrated should they come across two hides at the same time. Later on, when the dogs are very focused, these types of close hides

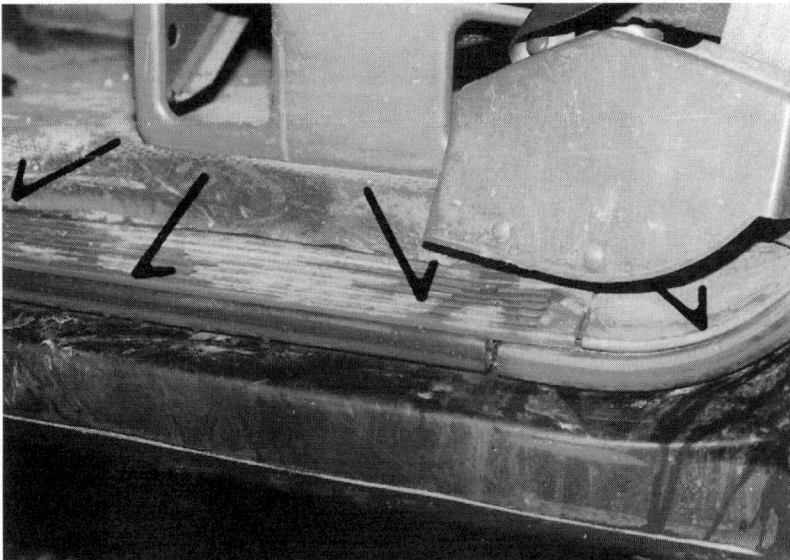

The newer the vehicle, the harder it will be for the dog to indicate the presence of explosives. The rubber door seals are firmer and have not lost their shape due to the regular opening and closing of the doors.

Make sure the dog checks the low areas first. This is the most logical area, because scent falls. But remember to check all areas, as air currents can affect the scent, or the bomber may have left explosive residue behind on the door frame or handles.

can be done more for the handler's benefit. At the beginning each car can have its own hide so that the dog gets greater vehicle exposure in the short time. Now proceed as before, right to left, low/high.

This whole process is done in about two days and gives each team a high degree of competency in such a short time. Now the handler/dog teams know how to search vehicles and

Have the dog check doors like these in a systematic fashion. Start with the cracks and work your way across to the hinges as the next most likely area.

These areas can be checked very quickly if you have a good search system. This may look like a lot to search, but with practice and good search habits, it becomes an easy task to complete.

where to investigate. I do the training in this manner because it breaks down the training process into two easy steps; the underside first and the doors and trunk lids second. There is not an overwhelming amount of small and narrow areas combined with the larger areas to check each and every time you set out to do some training, expecting each handler/dog team to remember and do the exercises with precision. It is a two-day, smooth flowing and effective way to train. It takes away the confusion because there is a lot for the handler/dog teams to learn and to remember each day. It is not books but hands-on practice that makes this so challenging. When I was taught explosive detection with Arco, it was not the step by step method that I now use for new and senior trainees. I was taught to get right into the matter, outside and inside searches on vehicles all at one time. Arco was already trained in Germany for explosives and I still had a very difficult time understanding if and when the dog was indicating a weak source of explosive scent or some other odorous item. I was taught to figure this out for myself. This became very frustrating for me and my trainer would never tell me until I could do no more with the dog because he began to false sit due to me frustrating him. My trainer was Brian Amm and he was a tough trainer. But I will admit I didn't quit, I continued to ask a lot of questions and as a result, I decided later on when I became the trainer that I would develop a system that would help the trainer use his/her time training handlers in the most efficient and effective way possible and to make training for handlers a complete learning experience that included fun, understanding the dog's characteristics or body actions at an early stage during training, and learning how to problem solve the little mistakes and nuances that do happen throughout the course of the day. So far I have not seen better results anywhere else and these comments have all come back from experienced dog handlers and commanders. What everyone sees in handlers/dog teams who have taken part in this course is a high level of confidence that is usually only seen with senior handlers and their dogs.

Whether or not your car/truck searches are done outdoors or indoors, trainers should always be planning ahead for training sites and always making the scenarios as challenging as possible. Make them fun because if it is fun the teams will learn more. The police garage or the police impound lots are the best sites for vehicle searches. In either location, vehicles come in a wide range of wear and tear and models. Vehicles at either of these locations are most usually parked side by side in long rows. To set up a training scenario here, pick one very long row of vehicles (20 or more) for each trainee where three different hides can be hidden. Make sure the vehicles are in relatively good shape or driveable. If you don't have enough vehicles for the amount of trainees to train on, then choose vehicles in groups of five or six for each trainee to search. Now set out three different hides, one on the engine, one in the passenger area and one in the trunk. Make sure that each handler has at least six vehicles to search so that each team has to put on a good effort to find the hides. The hides should weigh more than half a pound and the soak time should be more than one hour.

Assign one handler/dog team per set of six cars, three of which will have a designated hide. Make all of these unknown too; however, should a handler/dog team be having problems, still remind them from time to time when they are getting close to a hide. Set out the parameters for each scenario as the handler/dog teams come up to search, i.e., tell each handler a story of a crime. Tell them as if you are the investigating officer and that a certain car is believed to be the suspect vehicle. Now have the handler assess the call and the vehicle that is to be searched. As soon as he/she has assessed, ask them how they are about to search the vehicles. If the handler states that, as per the information he/she received, the search will begin with the suspect vehicle, stop them and suggest the system they should be using. First, no matter which vehicle the hide vehicle is:

1. Always work into the suspect vehicle. Never go directly to the suspect vehicle to begin the search. It may not be the right vehicle as suggested by the officers at the scene; or each time this is suggested to you and a hide is found you may be creating a problem later on down the road. What could start to happen is that the dog will after a while begin to sit at all the vehicles it is commanded to search. So, rather than create a problem, create some fun for the dog and make it work for its reward.

2. Make sure the handler uses the wind to his/her advantage when the search starts. Tell the handler to work into the wind when he/she sends the dog off on the cursory search. Have the handlers run their dogs along the fronts of the vehicles or along the backs of the vehicles; whichever end first will depend upon the direction the wind is coming from. As soon as the dog gets interest, have the handler move up with the dog into the area and either let the dog work it out with some encouragement or have them start a systematic of the vehicles right in that vicinity.

3. However, should nothing be indicated during the cursory then instruct the handlers to complete a systematic search of all the vehicles in that given sector and to start it into the wind.

4. If the search is done indoors, have the handlers make note of intake vents and hot air or air conditioning vents during their assessments. As soon as the handler tells you his/her assessment, have them tell you how the search will be done and where it will begin. The handler should tell you first a cursory search will be completed along the fronts of the vehicles and then along the backs of the vehicles. If nothing is found, then a complete and systematic search will be done on each of the vehicles starting at one end and ending at the other end.

The strength of the air being sucked up or blown out of an air vent can create disastrous problems for the search team.

The same goes for outdoor searches. Winds can create havoc for the teams involved, so make sure that you as the trainer are watching for signs the dog may be indicating so that the handler will be ready and to let the handlers know what is likely to happen and help each trainee out as they come into these problems. It's all about learning.

This is one reason the cursory search is such a valuable tool. In slightly windy conditions a cursory search can help the team narrow the search area down to a few vehicles. What can be observed by the handler as he/she stands back as the dog works most likely will not be so obvious if they are working close to the dog on a systematic search. It speeds the search up and makes the situation in the handler's mind a whole lot clearer. If the dog duly notes nothing, then the handler/dog team can begin their right to left/low-high searches.

Getting back to winds for a moment, they can create some very interesting but not insurmountable problems. In some of the outdoor searches, I witnessed two similar incidents in two different areas of the country. The scenario was a search of a set of vehicles, one of which was suspected of having explosives inside. It wasn't known which vehicle it was in. The dogs in each of the cases were sent first on the cursory searches and it was on these searches that both dogs made their indications that an explosive was nearby. However, the source could not be narrowed down. After a few long minutes of searching both dogs indicated and confirmed the presence of the explosive at a vehicle downwind from the hide vehicle. In both cases the handlers were really confused because the dogs were sitting in the middle of four parked vehicles, one of which had the hide. In both cases there was a wind. In one city it was late winter and it was a cool -2 or so, and in the other city it was -8 degrees. The winds were approximately NW at 5 km/hr. In each of the cases the dogs stayed in the central core area, never leaving it but for some reason never being able to find the source by going into the wind.

In the case of the Calgary member, the area was worked over and over again by the dog without the handler's help. This was good to see because the handler was not interfering and was really trying hard to observe everything that his dog was doing. The dog spent a lot of time checking another vehicle downwind of the hide vehicle. This handler, although not new to street work, was new to explosive detection and this was probably where experience would have alerted him to do a few things a little better. The Winnipeg dog handler, who had the experience and who I admire for his quick thinking, was able to understand what was going on. Both handlers stated they knew that the hide was close by. However, the difference between experience and no experience is a statement given by the Winnipeg handler, "I know it's here and because of the wind direction I know it's not in those two cars" (the downwind cars). He was right. But his dog was already tired from the search it had done in trying to locate the source. So was the Calgary dog. Both dogs did extremely well on their own and no one could have asked for more from either of the dogs.

These two handlers needed some additional help. As the instructor I asked the two handlers the same questions;

1. Could the hide be in that far row upwind of us? **A. No**

2. Judging by where the wind is coming from and the location of where the dog sat, its confirmation, could the hide be in the two cars on either side of our present location? (The two vehicles downwind of the hide vehicle.) **A. No**

3. In your mind, what is the only thing left to do? **A. Complete a better search (systematic) of the two cars here but particularly that one (hide vehicle).**

Both made very good decisions.

The teams had problems for two reasons. First, the colder temperatures kept the scent cone very close to the ground. The hides in each case were sizable hides of over three pounds in weight comprised of RDX and PETN placed on the floor of the passenger area. The hides had soaked for over two hours. Second, the strong wind was bouncing off of and swirling around four vehicles but particularly in the center area where the four cars met. One handler used his experience to think the process through while the other became experienced.

During the course of any search that a team is involved with, I am always asking the handlers questions pertaining to their search and I have them answer me without stopping the search and without taking their eyes off of their dogs. Why? First, it is because they are learning something while they are actually working and second, these are usually the times that the dogs are most likely to do something that would indicate to the handler that something is close by. But if the handler is looking back to the trainer or stops the search just as the dog is picking up the scent cone, then these things become negatives. Remember that an assessment does not only occur before each search, an assessment should be ongoing during the search. An assessment should be a constant thing.

In my mind vehicle searches are the most dangerous search or venue for the handler/dog teams. Car bombs are synonymous with biker turf wars or fundamentalist groups that thrive on terrorism. Until a bomb tech can get inside of one, no one knows how much explosive is inside, if any at all; no one knows when it will detonate or how it is designed to detonate the explosive. It is all very unnerving and dangerous.

How would one go about investigating such a vehicle or, for that matter, why would you want to? Why can be answered by just stating that it is in the public's interest, that if the occasion did arise, you would want to check to make sure that either the vehicle is or isn't loaded with explosives. If it were, then at least someone could get the ball rolling by getting as many of the public away from the scene as possible to prevent deaths and/or injuries. As for how would one do the search, I would have to say that this would be dictated by the situation itself. There is no stated "right way" of doing a search such as this. However, it can be done in a safe manner.

The only safe solution in doing a search such as this is to do it at a safe and discreet distance. How far is safe and discreet? The handler should be no closer than 500 yards if it is physically allowed. The dog can be directed into the wind and commanded to search the vehicle. Now going into the wind towards a vehicle with a large amount of explosives will probably not create any great excitement for the dog from the start. However, as the dog nears the vehicle, the handler will be observing some very fast and very strong changes in the body language and its indications. As the dog nears, the head should come straight up and fast. The ears will be set hard and forward. The head will be constantly stretching towards the sky and the dog will be picking up its speed towards the vehicle. The handler and everyone else watching will witness these changes. As the dog nears the vehicle, it may become confused by the huge amount of scent coming from the vehicle and just keep circling it to figure out what is so strange about this vehicle. The handler is probably thinking, why has the dog not sat on its own? but the fact remains that the dog may not sit or it may eventually sit. In most cases it will eventually sit.

The handler and everyone else there will probably be saying, "The dog should have sat." Like I said, they eventually do, but every once in awhile, the dog will come across a huge amount of explosive and if it has not practiced on large quantities, it will become confused because the odor is extremely overwhelming. To train for something like this is relatively easy. However, before you start training for this aspect, be sure that the dog is competent in all of the other areas. This aspect of training should be considered last because the dogs are at this point confident in themselves. This aspect of explosive searches is perhaps the biggest reason I support off line searching. The dogs have no problems working independent of the handler and the only thing left to teach these dogs is that it is okay to be searching 500 yards or more away from the handler. On line searching teams would have to approach the vehicle together and in this real life scenario, DO NOT GO UP WITH YOUR DOG TO INVESTIGATE. All that has to be done is to train your dog to go up on its own while the handler is outside the immediate danger area.

To begin your training set up the exercises with your bomb techs. See if it is possible to set up five or six cars at their practice range. Vehicles can be obtained from your local impound lot. These are vehicles that are destined for auction and therefore make excellent training venues. Set the vehicles up in the field end to end and side by side. It may seem a waste of time to set the vehicles up in these two fashions, but this set up is as much for the handler as it is for the dog. If these vehicles can remain at the range for a week or more, then the handler/dog teams and the trainer will accomplish a great deal.

In one of the vehicles place a hide either in the trunk or in the passenger area – front or back. The amount of explosive used for the hide should be a minimum of 50 pounds. If more can be obtained the better it will be for the trainees and the dogs. You will probably have a hard time justifying the use of over 50 pounds of military explosive, so use commercial explosives such as TNT or PETN or any other type. You can for interest's sake make the hides all unknown or you can make them known. I don't think, at this stage and with the amount of explosive used, that it really matters.

Choosing to search into the wind or at right angles to the wind or with the wind is entirely up to you as the trainer. Your experiences in the military or some other city, state, provincial or federal agency may have taught you to search at right angles to the wind, for example. You decide. However, one day, reality will have set in and you will have wished that you had practiced searching in all directions. I prefer searching into the wind because I know before my dog even gets there that something very big is in one of those vehicles. I can then prepare myself very early as to the next step I will take. So for me it is a matter of speed. If the dog indicates the vehicle quickly, that is efficiency. When the dog confirms soon thereafter, then that is effectiveness. Now the bomb techs can take over the rest of the scene. I also realize that searching into the wind may not be an option because of the physical make up of the scene. That will happen a lot. So practice your searching in all directions.

In order to get your dog to search at great distances from the handler, start at the half way mark – 250 yards (228 m). For the beginner dog the handler will search into the wind as much as possible, however I think you will find that the dog will be searching both into the wind and at right angles to the wind.

Sometimes it is not so easy for departments to get that many vehicles at one time. Therefore, if you can only obtain two or three vehicles, then so be it. Place these vehicles in a semi-circle, but still allowing the minimum 500-yard safety zone. As above, make one of the vehicles the hide vehicle, start at 250 yards, sending the dog into the wind.

Practice; practice this until the dog is good at this distance. You will from time to time be tested by the dog but keep pushing on. You may also at times find yourself having to get a little closer to the dog to make it obey a command or to just give it some moral support because the amount of scent is too overwhelming. This does work well, but like anything else it takes work and a whole lot of patience. Your department may not support such a move but one has to look at the overall picture and say, it is necessary because of what you do and how you do it may save a whole lot of lives.

c) Heavy Equipment

There is nothing extra special to mention here that has not been already mentioned. I use heavy equipment because they are excellent venues to teach the dogs on. They are big so the dog has lots of area to search and there is a lot of air contaminating scents coming from these machines, such as heavy oils, diesel fuel and dirt, which makes it all the more challenging for the dogs. If they are available, then use them.

3. Air Terminals

During 1996/97, most Canadian International Air Terminals switched over from federal policing (RCMP) to municipal or regional policing. Most of the departments were faced with an added dimension of policing, Explosive Detection Dogs (EDDs), which the majority did not have. Suddenly there was a rush to secure dogs, additional staff and a course training standard that met all of the requirements of Transport Canada and Emergency Planning, who regulate and govern all aspects of airline and passenger safety at international terminals.

At the time no one knew what those requirements were, because most of the departments involved had never before worked under federal jurisdiction rules. Basically, the federal government had to that point contracted out its own police force to supply the bomb sniffing dogs, the training and yearly validations of each dog, and to develop a Standard Operating Procedure and a Course Training Standard. What the RCMP Dog Unit developed was excellent and, although amended over the years, is still being used by the RCMP today. Transport Canada also supplied all of the x-ray technology and explosive vapor detectors, better known as EVDs. As soon as the RCMP left the terminals, the various agencies had to acquire explosives dogs and handlers. The Airport Authorities were responsible for the takeover or purchase of new x-ray technology and the EVDs. They were also responsible for contracting municipal, regional and federal police departments to secure the air terminals. They also contracted private security firms to assist with the simple aspects of securing an air terminal. Police departments were finding themselves in a new role of police management in that they were being contracted to fulfill the role of armed security at the airports. This brought about sharp changes within the structure of the police departments, because they now found themselves having to disrupt the regular street patrol units so that they could fill the positions posted for airport duty as per the contract signed with the airport authorities. That meant additional costs to the departments for vehicles, office space and EDDs. As if this wasn't bad enough, the police services had to equip their dog units with additional vehicles, explosive storage facilities at the airports, as well as purchasing the EDDs and setting up a Standard Operating Procedures Manual and a Transport Canada accredited Course Training Standard for the dogs and their handlers. This was not a big undertaking, but nonetheless, in typical police management fashion, everything was started when the program was to have been already in place. In some cases, police managers would be telling their dog units that they (the police department and EDD unit) were not going to be responsible for the airport's EDD program, and the airport authority would be telling the officer in charge of the unit that they would be beginning the program and that funds were in fact already there. The bureaucrats were playing politics again. The commander of the dog section didn't even know that all of this was going on in Calgary. This goes to show you just how important the security of the public, passengers, flight crews and airline owners is to some police departments.

This is why this section of the book is going to have an excellent breakdown of what should be done and how it should be done. Are our International Air Terminals in Canada safe from terrorist attacks, domestic and foreign? Do we take airport security seriously? No, we do not. In the United States, at least when I have had the opportunity to travel through, people take a more serious approach towards security. It is not only easy for terrorist groups to gain admittance, even citizenship, to Canada, it is frighteningly easy for members of these groups to get jobs with airports that allow them free and easy access to all areas of the airport and aircraft. The sad part is that when something does happen, innocent travelers will get hurt or die and the police departments will get most of the blame. This is why the police should have a top-notch course.

Secondly, are the budgets needed to sustain a police-secured presence at the airports adequate? It is extremely costly. Airport authorities have to find funds for contracting police and security, specialty squads such as EDDs, vehicles and so on. That in itself can be in the millions of dollars, depending on how grand the scheme of things will be. That is just the tip of the iceberg. There are also building costs, employees and Hi-Tech equipment such as x-ray machines and the EVDs (explosives vapor detectors). These Hi-Tech pieces are very expensive. They are also very unreliable.

Transport Canada personnel may read this book and say that I have a biased opinion in favor of dogs. They will also say that I am trying to get more business for myself by throwing out a few scares here and there. Nothing is further from the truth. I do endorse Hi-Tech equipment as long as it has a success rate of more than 20 percent. That means 80 percent of explosives or devices can get on board a flight without detection. I can back everything I'm saying with proof. This proof was also put into writing for those in charge of security for airport authorities. These reports were also given to Transport Canada personnel in Ottawa, who to this date still endorse cheaper, ineffective equipment that does not perform what it is supposed to.

When I am putting on seminars or training sessions for airport police departments, I include everyone during the training scenarios. Why? I do this because searching suspicious luggage or packages is not just about EDDs and their handlers. It's about the team. Everyone involved with the security of the airport, police, security at the various gates and airport authority management, is the whole team. To be successful, the team has to be cohesive, otherwise efficiency, effectiveness and safety are just three words thrown around to impress people that everything that can be done is being done. Let me explain what I mean.

All training scenarios that were set up had to include, at the very beginning, the private security people who manned the x-ray machines and metal detectors at the gates. I had the explosives (three different commercial explosives) placed into separate airtight plastic kits, which were placed in among other items in a carry bag. The hides were to be in a pre-boarding waiting area. But before I could get through, I had to pass through the gate passenger check area. I would place the carry-on bag (that already had a luggage tag on the handle) among the other passengers' bags onto the conveyor belt into the x-ray machine without being noticed. Because I had a security tag on, all I had to do was to keep walking to the other end of the machines and wait for the bag to come through. As it came through, I noticed the viewing screen was on black and white mode.

I didn't tell anyone there what I was doing other than waiting for the handlers to come in with their dogs for training. The bag came through and slid down the ramp to the collector where I just picked it up. The bag was not picked to be opened, even though they had all watched it go by.

I then asked the supervisor if she wanted to see some actual explosives go through the x-ray device. When she looked at my bag her face turned white. It wasn't their fault at all. They hadn't been shown all of the different types of explosives that are available on the market. I asked why they didn't look at the bag any further, to which they all said that the items inside of the bag looked like cans of food or candles and there were no wires to be seen. So why bother to pull it off. I then had them put the screen onto color mode. I put the carry-on case through again. The explosive and anything else that was organic came through a bright orange. I asked if they would have taken a better look inside the case if that were what they were seeing. Some said they would and others said no. The reason for it was that these particular explosives looked like soup cans and a lot of the passengers on the domestic flights sometimes carry food in their bags, so it was not out of the ordinary. But the big thing for them was the fact that no wires were seen. Another security member gave me a very interesting comment. He said, "You know, of all the training we have had, if we were to look for an explosive, we wouldn't be looking for something that looked like this. We would be looking for something that resembled sticks, because that is what they use to check up on us from time to time. I have never seen anything that looks like this." I found that to be very interesting.

I then explained to them that explosives come in shapes of pillows, soup cans, sticks, prills and powder form. However, I also stated to them they shouldn't depend upon the fact that because no wires were seen that it didn't mean that the components to make a bomb were not there. It could mean that the components, i.e., batteries, were already in the CD player and the wires and detonator were elsewhere. I did show them and they were very surprised. For obvious reasons I won't divulge that part of the conversation in this book, but it was easy to accomplish because of the way they were taught to search people and until they change the way they are taught to search, it will be a sure way of getting the components on a flight.

Another bothersome thing was mentioned to me. As security checkpoint personnel, they are required to keep the passengers pumping through the gates, especially at peak times. However, there had been a few incidents with a few of the airline directors, who were catching a flight back to a head office or whatever. As these security people would be checking through some of the passengers' luggage as they are supposed to, a few of these airline bosses would go to the front of the line and ask point blank, "What's the reason for the slow down? Let the passengers through, enough of this silliness." Now here are a group of people who should be promoting airline safety instead of giving a $10.00 an hour security attendant a hard time for doing a job he is supposed to do as per Transport Canada regulations.

Now if we talk about the baggage that gets checked in at the ticket counter and is sent on its way downstairs or out back to be loaded onto the aircraft, that's a different story. None of these pieces get checked at all unless it is requested that a dog check the entire load or a few pieces because of an ongoing police investigation. However, there is a machine that acts like a vacuum cleaner, sucking all the air in and around a pallet full of luggage into an explosive vapor detection machine. There is a simple way of getting past this machine too, which again I will not divulge for obvious reasons.

So why wouldn't Transport Canada want to make sure that the security personnel have the best training possible and not the less-than-basic course that is given to them now? These people want to do a good job and feel really silly when someone like me comes along. That is why every chance I get to train at any airport, I will always include the security personnel. They actually enjoy it and feel it is important.

Second, I set out the explosives in various areas in the pre-boarding locations. The usual soak time is allowed and we are ready to go. In this segment I have the police personnel come in with their EVDs. Everyone is on standby, the second EVD and the dog handlers. The EVD Teams go through first.

They check every possible thing that can be checked. The whole area was checked with these machines in approximately 30 minutes with no hits. In actual fact, this was one of the documented cases that was sent to Transport Canada's office in Ottawa. There were three hides of no less than one pound and no more than five pounds. Both operators of these machines got to within a few inches of the hides and nothing registered. Yet, each operator completed all of the mechanical pre-testing on these machines, which indicated that they were in proper working order. When I told the officers that they all were at the hides with their machines, but didn't register the find, the comments were "that doesn't surprise us. That's why we refuse to trust them." The dogs are the answer because they are 100 percent right on all the time.

The dogs were brought out next. Each dog worked one at a time, but with its own section of the lobby areas. Time combined for both dogs, for the same total area that was completed by the operators and their machines, was under six minutes. This is a large area that has hundreds of seats, a lot of garbage receptacles, phone booths, play areas for children, washrooms, computer stations at all the gates that have numerous drawers and so on. This is a busy place to search. One of the major differences between the EVD operators and the handlers with their dogs was simply that the EVD operator was never taught (at that time) to properly search a room or an aircraft. They were never taught to assess the call or the setting that is to be searched. The only reason for this is because so much faith is put into these Hi-Tech machines. This faith is a false sense of security and it is dangerous.

Let's recap all of the pros and cons of each of the above:

- You have security personnel at the gates who did not investigate the carry case because on the black and white screen they did not see any wires to indicate a bomb.
- On the color screen they saw dark orange that indicated an organic substance, but the shape of the explosive made it look like food items and they let it go by.
- On occasion airline management personnel have tried to intimidate gate security personnel to speed things up, calling the searches questionable.

- Gate security personnel want to be involved with the scenario training because they feel what has been taught to them is not enough.
- The mountain of evidence is that EVDs do not properly work most of the time and that the operators refuse to put any kind of faith in them.
- The EVD operators are not trained to search efficiently or effectively.

These are all the cons.

As for the pros of the above, there are none. This is all about a false sense of security that exists within all of our international airports to this very day. It also says that Transport Canada, Airport Authorities and most Police Service Managers feel that this is Canada and that nothing will happen here because nothing has ever happened in our peaceful nation, which the whole world loves. Well, I hate to burst everyone's bubble, but mysterious mishaps have happened because of Canada. They have either happened domestically, or originated in Canada then happened elsewhere in the world. The bombing in Japan, where a baggage worker was killed, is believed to have originated in Canada and the bombing of an Air India flight is also suspected to have originated in Canada. That is why my feelings for the EDDs are so strong. They do work, you can train for perfection, although perfection cannot be found anywhere in the world of anything that exists. However, if you can achieve a 99.9 percent success rate, then that to me is as close to perfection as you can get and it should be strived for. My other concern is for the EDD Units, be they at the airports or on the street. If anything does go wrong due to a manager's incpt way of thinking, or because they are better paper pushers than they are commanders, no matter how well the handler/dog teams work or how efficient they are, the dog unit will always pay the price in most cases. If an incident does happen at an airport somewhere in Canada, and perhaps even in the U.S., fault will be lavished upon the police department's standard of training and the EDD Unit in question. The sad part is that upper police management will also question the unit for any mishap, without any support to the handlers and their dogs, and the handlers themselves will shoulder all the guilt because of a mishap. This is way too much to put on anyone's shoulders. These people do not get enough pay for these situations.

With the above in mind, the following information is a plan of what I taught to the Calgary Police Service Dog Unit/EDD Course and to the Winnipeg Police Service Dog Unit/EDD Course. The trainers were taught how to train their handlers to work Efficiently, Effectively and with Safety in mind. The trainers were also taught how to prepare search scenarios that would include the gate security personnel and the police officers at the air terminals as well as the EVD operators. The order of training venues at the air terminals is also very important. The air terminal has a high density of movement of people and vehicles and is very noisy. I begin the training with a step by step formula of areas or venues. In order of importance, the following training venues are to be completed over a period of three to four weeks.

1. Pre-boarding waiting areas
2. Baggage holding and loading areas
3. Cargo sheds
4. Aircraft, inside and outside searches.

1. Pre-Boarding Waiting Areas

Before any training with dogs begins in these areas, I always walk through these areas with the handlers. These areas, depending upon how big the air terminal is, can range from 50 feet wide by 100 feet long to three or four times the size. Inside of these areas are numerous garbage receptacles, passenger seats, washrooms and gate attendant counters that have large numbers of drawers, boxes and cupboards contained in these units. Also included in these areas are numerous information booths of various designs and configurations. In all, it is a lot to comprehend when a new handler is watching his/her dog, the areas being searched and passengers watching them.

When you enter such an area, stand back and look at its size. Tell the handlers that no matter what they are intending to do, be it training or a real call, never rush in to do the work. Always assess the area, making note of the following:

a) Size. If the area is a large area, break it down into workable sections. Look for markers where you will end that section of the search. Markers can be the last row of seats, a pillar or newspaper box, or where the carpet meets the tiled floor.

b) Content. Envision each section and take note of what is in the area. Look at the section as a small part of the whole and ask where the quickest and best place would be to place a small device. As you look at the picture there are two possibilities, garbage receptacles and, if in the section, washrooms. These would be the first things to search.

Why? There are several reasons, but I always try to put it into the concept of efficiency and effectiveness. First I take into account that my thick haired partner is going to become exhausted in a short time because the air inside of the air terminal is very hot and dry. So I want to complete the whole search in the quickest (efficient) but also in the most productive (effective) manner possible. In the past, I have observed trainers teach the handlers to complete the searches of the whole area without even giving the handlers a chance to think out the search systematically. I have observed trainers watch the teams search to the point where it was pointless for the handlers to be there with their dogs. Handlers were short tempered and the dogs were becoming very tired. It was a bummer of a training session and contrary to their own belief, the handlers and dogs learned nothing. It is because the trainers themselves did not know how to search efficiently and effectively. This was especially evident when the dogs completely searched everything else in the room more than once, and then the dogs were directed to search the tall garbage receptacles, that all of this became evident. If a hide were placed inside of a garbage receptacle and the dogs were commanded to search them, several things would happen, all of which would be the handler's fault for the dog's problems. If the receptacles were quite high, they would likely fall over from the weight of the dog. Already tired and its tongue hanging out, this dog wants no part of a tipping garbage can. Now try to get it up another and another. Or, the dog does get up to the opening and he places his nose over top, then gets back down to go to the next item of search, and the handler finds out later that there was in fact a hide inside. Well, why in heaven's name didn't you help the handler out? Why is there another downer for the team? The tired dog and tipping garbage receptacles is a common occurrence and so are trainers whose only focus is to make sure the dogs get the odors and sit.

I teach the handlers and trainers alike, that when you enter into these areas you will do two things first. First do a cursory search, then in a systematic fashion search all garbage containers before anything else. Garbage containers offer bombers quick hiding places. If you have only seats and garbage containers, why would you want to tire the dog out searching the seats first? Search the garbage cans first. Then if there are washrooms, do them next. When that is all done, complete the room in a left/right fashion and then go on to the next. Follow the same system all of the time. If you get a system going it becomes like clockwork to check these items first. Nothing is missed.

As an added safety, I also have another handler in waiting to be the searching handler's back-up. Should anything be missed, and it is not impossible, the number two man can be the eyes and at the end of the search just tell the number one handler that a spot was missed. I do not believe in re-searching the whole area with the dog again. It is wasted energy and is a downer for the team. The dogs and the handlers will be good enough as long as the course permits it and the trainer builds upon the team's confidence.

With garbage receptacles, there are some things that can be done to avoid problems:

● The common problem with all garbage containers is that dogs do not get their noses deep enough inside. While searching for explosives we certainly do not want to get into the habit of having to tip the receptacle over so the dog can get a good sniff. Unfortunately, that is exactly what has to be done sometimes if the handler's dog is short in stature. Depending upon the height of the container and the amount of explosive inside, having the dog put its nose over the top of the opening is not going to be good enough. If the hide is two to five pounds, then your dog will get a good sniff, especially if it is a container located outside. But for indoor searches the dog will not get enough. The other common problem is that the dogs quite often tip the cans over. For the big German Shepherds, their size usually pushes the can forward, while the smaller dogs such as Labradors tend to pull it back to them and over while they are trying to reach inside. Is this a dilemma? No, just a minor problem that requires a minor adjustment to remedy the situation. When the handler gets the dog to jump up, just hang onto the garbage container without getting into the dog's space and let it do the work. If the handlers continue to allow the dog to pull or push the garbage receptacles down, the problem will manifest itself to the point where the dog will refuse to get onto the garbage containers.

● Another method is to put enough explosive inside of the container that after 30 minutes of soak time the dog will get enough scent that will entice it to put its head deeper into the receptacle that will allow the dog to get a stronger amount of explosive scent into its olfactory system. Continue with this method of training, using large amounts of odorous garbage to try to throw the dog off. However, be careful here. With food, and especially with Labradors being totally in love with scraps of food, make sure the handler is able to tell the difference between the dog indicating food and an explosive hide. This can be extremely deceiving to some handlers as these types of dogs show very similar signs. It is a knack that does take time to know and with some dogs it takes handlers a lot of work and patience.

● For those hides that appear between the container itself and the garbage bag, these take some smart thinking. If the garbage receptacle does not have a lid or cover, the dog should, without much problem, find the hide between the two as long as it is directed there. However, with those containers that are enclosed with a lid, getting the dog to search in between the garbage bag and the container is a problem in itself. You have to remove the lid so that access can be gained to allow the dog to get at the scent. Unless there is residue on the outer edge of the bag, the dog will have a very difficult time indicating any scent at all. I realize that this is something that your bomb techs may not endorse, but it is the only way around this problem. We don't always have the perfect situation at our disposal and therefore we have to improvise and adapt.

As stated above, trainers should increase the size of the search areas and increase the degree of difficulty for each handler to make it challenging.

2) Baggage Holding/Loading Areas

Transport Canada states that dogs must be able to search 300 pieces of baggage an hour. This is a suggested quantity and, as far as I know, is not written in stone. However, they seem too fixated on numbers and these are numbers that were given to me. A member of the Security and Emergency Planning Group of Transport Canada stated to me that if the dog was not capable of searching 300 bags an hour then it was of no use and that x-ray machines and vapor machines would be used. How arrogant. This is another way of saying the machines are superior. Once again, at least in Canada, they are not. Their success rate is still in the 30% range and that is not good enough. Someday the machines will be much more accurate, but for now nothing touches the dog's ability.

The dog too does not come without its shortcomings. However, its shortcomings are due to the human factor. The F.A.A. also has its expected total numbers of pieces a dog must do in one hour. I am not able at this time to give those numbers, and as is the case with Transport Canada, they too may be only suggested numbers and not be written in stone. Whatever the case may be, I do not have a problem with these numbers, as they are only numbers. What I am always concerned about is the safety of those flying and of those loading the aircraft. Three hundred bags an hour per dog, is it safe? That question has bothered me personally since the member of Transport Canada stated that if the dog cannot search 300 pieces an hour, then it is not wanted. Costly machines will be used. That is fine. As I stated all along, I have no problems with machines as long as they do what they say they can do.

The trace elements that these machines detect is in the parts per million. The dog's nose is significantly stronger. That means that there must always be some trace elements on the outside of the luggage before the machine can detect. If the trace elements are too small an amount to check, then the machine will not check or acknowledge the explosive. A dog, on the other hand, will investigate and in most cases will eventually sit to confirm and in a few instances will cause the handler to be very curious and have the bag pulled off anyway. The machine cannot do that at all. What everyone is saying is that there must be some residue on the outside of the luggage for the dogs and machines to find. Eventually, there will be a bomber/terrorist who is smart enough not to leave any traces at all. At the speed the dog has to go, locating such a bag is next to impossible. If we look at all the different bags or pieces of luggage that are available on the market today, and depending upon the size of the hide, the dog will have an exceptionally difficult time with it and as for the machines, nil. Unless there is a miracle machine out in the world, the machine will not find it at all.

Along with some of the members of the Calgary Police Service Dog Unit, I did do some testing with the handlers and their dogs with regards to large amounts inside of suitcases that are commonly used throughout the world. Inside the suitcase was over ten pounds of TNT BASE explosive. It was specifically chosen because of its strong odor, but was not as strong as the NG BASE explosives. The explosive was placed between the clothing and had a soak time of about a half a day. I was very careful not to get any trace elements or contamination on the outside of the suitcase, especially on the handle.

The suitcase then went through the regular route as it would normally go, down the chute to the back loading area and onto a cart. The cart that was being loaded was for luggage that was not being loaded for another five hours. The baggage attendants knew of the training and set the five buggies aside for us to take off and place on the flat revolving carousel. There were well over 200 bags on these carts. Everyone took part in loading the luggage onto the carousel as it moved and the handler went about searching the luggage with his dog. The team moved as fast as they could, trying to cover all bags as they came on. It was very difficult for the team to keep up with the speed of the moving belt and the quickness of the bags being put onto the belt at specific distances. The hide was not located. Now, I thought the team did a very good job of searching and the dog (Lab) was exceptional, but nothing was found. This was all repeated but the search was done at a speed that was comfortable to the dog. The team did each piece in the fashion that they were taught to, handle/zipper or clasp area, four corners and latches, a simple procedure that covers all aspects of the luggage and in good time. When the dog approached the piece with the hide, he sniffed it energetically until it got to the latch area. It began to show specific interest but not enough to confirm but enough to cause the handler to take note and work more of the suitcase. It was not until the dog got to one of the corners that it took a very deep breath and then sat. Speed or 300 bags an hour should never be an issue; safety should.

My feelings on all of this: do what is right and what is best. The handler/dog teams should never fail a real call. If 300 bags an hour becomes an issue, then I have a simple solution – have two dogs do 150 bags an hour each and you will arrive at the 300 mark. I do not believe in 300 an hour and I therefore do not teach it. However, that is a choice that I made. Another department undoubtedly will make theirs. Know in your heart that it is the wise and safe choice. We are not here to please the personnel at Transport Canada or the F.A.A.; we are here to make it safe for our public.

Costs are one of the factors that all police departments or private security groups say hinder them from acquiring an EDD UNIT for the airports or street work. One dog that is pretrained on explosives with an eight week or so course costs approximately U.S. $7000. If the course can be held in the city where the unit resides, then there is additional savings from room and board. If the team has to go elsewhere, then there are the added costs of room and board. Depending upon how many teams are required, the initial costs are very low and you now have something that can be utilized for years to come. Dogs can effectively be used until they are eight or nine years old.

One of the things that I have done is to study the different types of carry-on bags and suitcases that exist today. It is phenomenal. Some are cheap as dirt and offer no resistance to the odor of the explosive. Others are very expensive and made to withstand water, dirt and anything else that may get inside and damage the clothing. Some have hard plastic shells, some are made of rip-stop canvas type materials with high porosity values and others with low porosity values, all of which can either make searching easy or make it difficult. So it is very important to know all of these things. It is important to know how your dog may react to these different elements. That is why I pay close attention to these little insignificant things. Believe it or not, but this information has been very valuable to me and to others over the years. No matter how tough a suitcase is made, a good dog will get the scent.

In preparation for training on luggage I think just about everyone has a good system from which they can gain great successes. Is there a right way or a wrong way? I can't answer that. There are only a few ways the scent can come out of a suitcase, so eventually you will train the dog to indicate the right suitcase. We also train the dogs to search 300 pieces an hour. Some departments like to train their dogs by contaminating the handles or other parts of the luggage with traces of explosive. There are also those who do not use very much explosives at all and depend a great deal on pseudo-explosive marking pens. I personally feel these pens are for those who do not have much insight into training and prefer the easy way out. These pseudo-markers offer that and only that. If anything at all, always practice with the real thing. There is no substitution.

STEP 1

To begin this part of the exercise, I went directly to the air terminal and obtained left behind luggage that had clothing inside. Choose one of the pieces to place a stick of C-4 in among the clothing. Lay out flat as many pieces of luggage as you can. The primary goal here is to get the dog to search luggage and to eventually find the hide. All of the pieces of luggage are left open, lids back and clothing exposed. This only takes a few repeats of three to four times and then the handler can go on to the next step. During this time I can determine which dog is going to bite

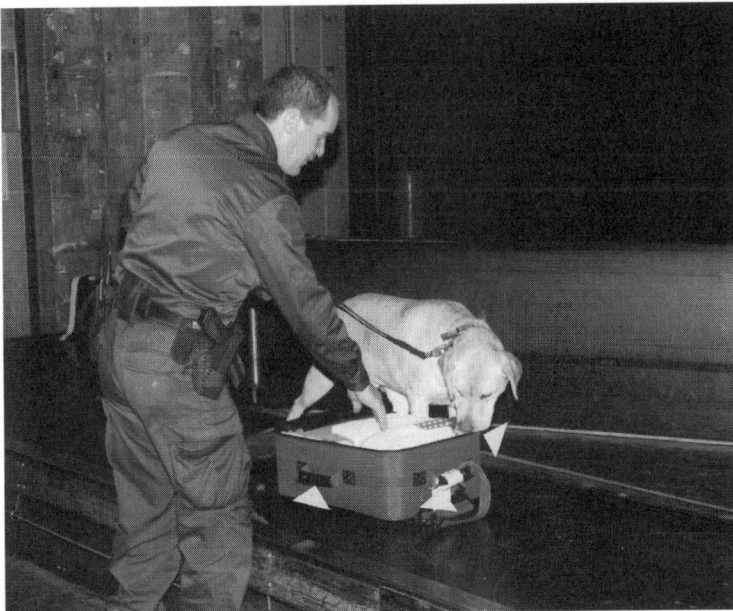

at the clothing, at which time there will be a correction. This is the time for the corrections and not later on. This system is also good for the laid back dog or mid-range to below mid-range dogs. Even though the luggage is open, the dogs can still be taught to search each and every corner. As I said, this part does not take long and you may feel that it is not necessary. However, remember that this is an introduction and a gauge for dogs. This can either be done on the floor, if a moving belt is not available, but if one is readily near, then use it. This will also tell you if your dog ignores the moving belt that it is walking on as it searches the luggage. If there any problems with the dogs, this first step should take the dog's mind off of the belt with the aid of the easy finds.

STEP 2

Depending upon the level of dog, this step can be done in two ways. First, if you have a weaker dog but he/she is still doing the work, you can now introduce the dogs to semi-closed luggage. That is, luggage with the lid flipped back over the clothing, but not closed. For the stronger dogs the lids can be flipped back over and partially closed. Most suitcases have zippers on them. Instead of always stopping the zipper at the handle, try stopping the zippers at each corner of the suitcase as well as the handle. Try to start the dog on the opposite of where the zipper is stopped. This will cause the dog to always look for the small opening while the search is on because it's never where it was the last time. Dogs have uncanny memory recall. Now the dog begins to look for the openings or the

places where the scent can be easily sniffed out. Continue using the same explosive, as these first two steps are all done in one day.

STEP 3

Step 3 is the last step to this system of luggage training. All luggage is closed. For the different types of luggage, determine different amounts of explosives. The weights or size of the explosives can range from a half pound to three to five pounds. As the trainer make sure that the pieces of luggage have a soak time of at least one hour. Practicing on moving belts or on the floor in a stationary position is very important. In one manner, i.e., the floor or stationary, the dogs have no distractions other than the workers or moving vehicles. Therefore, this is where I would start with the dogs before I moved to searching on the moving

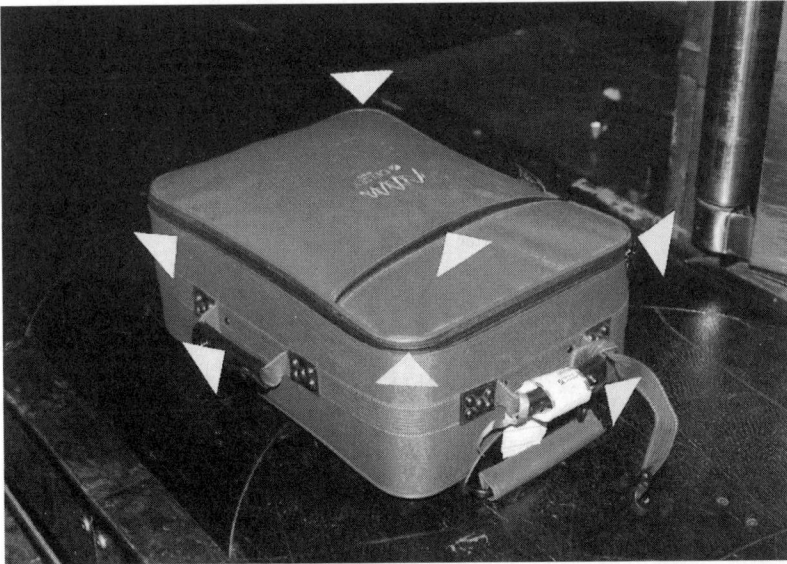

belt. Therefore the dog gets used to the numbers of suitcases it searches while the distractions are ongoing. For another, the handler is getting used to reading the dog and teaching it or showing it all of the spots to search on the pieces of luggage without the hindrance of the movement. If you start on the belt with a green dog and a green handler, you as a trainer are apt to have more problems and therefore have to extend training because of these problems. So it is simpler and yes, a little more work, but it is repetitious work from which the dog learns. By the time the floor or stationary searches are finished, the dogs will be ready for the belt or moving searches.

The dogs by this stage should have total focus on the luggage searching and if the movement of the belt should bother a dog or two, the desire to check the suitcases should override the distraction of the moving belt.

Make sure that hides are placed within the luggage, among all of the clothing and in the outside pockets as well. Mix everything up to create a higher level of interest. As I stated earlier in this chapter, be sure to have the availability of the different types of luggage to train on. THIS IS VERY IMPORT-ANT. To diversify, try leaving the luggage on the buggies and observe how well the dog and handler do with this type of searching. As a handler may find him/herself with this kind of situation, it is good to practice on, especially when that is exactly how packages are stacked, on pallets or trolleys.

Another important factor that I mentioned earlier is to train with contamination on the luggage and no contamination on the luggage. It is perhaps better to train without the contam-ination on the outside as one or two dogs out of a group just may decide that it is easier to look for the scent on the outside of the suitcase or carry-on bag as to really search for the scent through zippers and clasps. In other words, it may be a dangerous trend to make the searches for the dog too easy. Just be wise, is all I am saying.

OF INTEREST TO ALL TRAINERS: in areas or zones where the weather from season to season becomes extreme, be careful of where you set your training scenarios up, i.e., in air terminal luggage bays or near large cargo bay doors. When the temperatures are at extreme ends of the thermometer (outside to inside) be careful that the scent coming from the source is not sucked outside. Remember that if the temperature outside is 30 below and the temperature inside is 75 above, that is a difference of 105 degrees. So, if your hide or your scenario is close to a large bay door and a luggage jockey opens the large bay door and it is 30 below outside and 75 inside, what do you think will happen to the scent coming out from the source (suitcase)? I guarantee it will be sucked out the door. As a result, your trainees may have problems with the searches because there may not be any scent left. Now you have to let the hides soak for a few minutes more before the search begins.

3) Cargo Sheds (Packages)

Cargo is all about packages and envelopes. Some of the best venues to train at are of course air terminal cargo sheds, courier companies such as Purolator or Federal Express, or the stores and supplies areas of large municipal agencies. A trainer should have access and a contact at each of the locations so that training can be conducted with a high degree of realism. These are places where the environment is always changing day to day, which makes for excellent work. Set your training scenarios up at the sheds, inside of the aircraft itself and in trucks.

Begin with simple hides that are easy to locate. Because there are a lot of nooks and crannies within a relatively small area or pile of packages, the dog and handler have a lot to search in that area and it is easy to miss searching a package or two. Place the explosive inside of any size box and then place it into the pile along with the rest of the boxes and envelopes. Place the hides in such a manner that the dogs will get a variance of positions to seek out; i.e., one hide low and

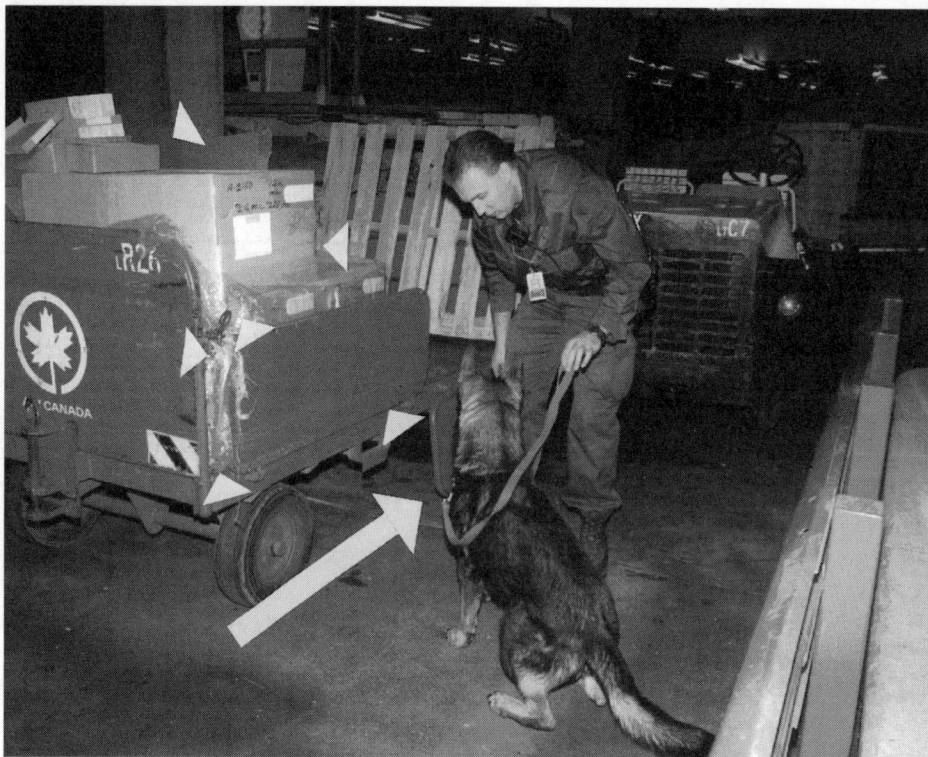

on the outside, another hide high and on the outside and another either low or high but on the inside.

Change the degree of difficulty from time to time. Place food in some of the boxes and place the explosive in with the food. Tape the boxes up and or wrap them in paper. With these types, make the hides the night before, making sure that the outside of the box does not become contaminated with explosive.

Begin the searches as you would a room, left to right, boxes on the floor first, then (if any) boxes on the next level up (high hides). This is only at a location such as a cargo shed. Usually at a courier's workplace, all cargo is at floor level with the exception of cargo placed in trucks. As you can see, any venue has its own peculiar characteristics. Each with its own persona, handlers and their dogs must be able to meet these little challenges by understanding what is different at each of these places and practice.

Being in Calgary has actually created a problem for our training as far as cargo searching is concerned. Calgary is a hub for head offices and oil field related equipment suppliers. With oil comes oil exploration, with oil exploration comes seismic and with seismic comes commercial explosives. A lot of these technicians do a lot of flying throughout the western provinces going from oil site to oil site. Explosives could be, and most likely are being, flown on regional aircraft into and from Calgary and Edmonton air terminals. At least twice a week, while training at the cargo sheds or at the luggage area at the terminal, either of the two bomb dogs at Calgary will sit/confirm at a bag or at a large tool-box at the cargo shed. Inside one carry-on bag clothing belonging to a member of a seismic crew was found. At the cargo sheds, the locked up large plastic tool chests contained something that had the odor of explosives or in fact had explosives inside.

Now, some might say that the dog is indicating and confirming something that has a very strong and confusing odor. Wrong; the way the dog reacted to the large plastic tool chest, there really was explosive odor inside. But it is up to the air carrier to open the chest and we as police officers were powerless without a warrant, and the items were leaving within the next two hours. It is not the seismic companies or the oil companies that transport the items; it is the workers or employees.

So what do you do with a dog that confirms at the chest, but you cannot confirm what is inside or is not? The problem I have with this is that the handlers, although I trained them, are probably the best and most efficient there are. They are true professionals. Second, both dogs are excellent. However, both confirmed in these situations. So what could we do? There was nothing that could be done. Airline personnel are reluctant to destroy locks on these items (especially when it's a training scenario and not a real call). I am retired from duty, so even though it had an impact on me, I could do nothing. These two guys were really and truly concerned, but because it was only training, and because of potential lawsuits and payment for damages, they could do nothing. So, should you be in an area where there is a lot of oil activity, be prepared for something like this. There should be transport regulations that prevent employees transporting explosive contaminated clothing and tools in aircraft. There should also be regulations that permit police to search such cargo without warrant in situations such as this. Airline companies in Canada are too trusting of their customers and therefore are not capable of making a sound judgement call when situations like this arise.

4) Aircraft/ Inside and Outside Searches

Although there is an abundance of places to search on an aircraft, the whole procedure can be accomplished with ease. The basis has already been introduced to the team during the bus searches. Begin at the front, assess, send the dog on a cursory or scan search to the back and then from the back to the front search all of the areas in a systematic fashion with a figure eight shaped low/high search of the seats and the overhead compartments.

Before any searching begins do an introductory assessment with all of the handlers first, showing them the most likely places to search first and the order of search or fashion that will be used. Indicate to the handlers that during a call or situation that no one else will be on the aircraft except for the search team. All doors will be closed except for the one at the front entrance to the aircraft. However, if the aircraft were situated away from the terminal on the tarmac, then I would suggest closing the door until the search with the dog has been completed. This is a discretionary call, but is recommended so as not to create any further air currents that may shift the pattern of the scent cone away from the dog's nose.

Be aware of circulating fans in the bathrooms and how they can effect the flow of the scent and where the dog is most likely to indicate the scent first. Make it known to the handlers that if the aircraft is parked away from the terminal after its last flight, the cleaning staff will come in to service the craft. If the hides are set out before they come then someone has to stay to guard the explosives until the cleaners have finished with their tasks. Also note that while the front door is ajar and the back service doors are open, the air rushing through will cause the scent cone to move around and possibly pool in areas that may cause the trainer and handler some confusion.

The cockpit is a "be careful zone." If searches are conducted here be extremely careful that the dog does not jump onto the console. This equipment is very expensive and delicate and this could cause some serious problems. If this does happen, let the chief engineer know of this so that he/she may send in a crew to check things out. Otherwise, the team need only search the first part of the cockpit up to the backs of the captain's and co-pilot's seats.

If it is at all possible, have the handler's number two man go ahead to retract the armrests located between the seats. This just takes a few moments while the handler does the assessment and it makes it easier for the dog to search the seats and the overhead bins. It is also important to show the handlers that the seats are floatation devices and can easily be lifted to hide an explosive, and that it is therefore crucial that the dog gets its head down low during the searches. It is also important to know that the newer materials used on the aircraft seats have an almost zero porosity level and that some of the magazine pouches on the newer aircraft require the dog to put its nose over top of the openings of the pouches before the dog can scent an explosive. These are all little, but very important things to remember that will help out with the training.

On the outside of the aircraft are several areas to search as well. These areas are less intricate but must be done. The cargo bays and the landing gear wells or receptacles can be easily searched by hand, however, there is still enough visual distraction within these wells that a hide of explosive could easily be missed. Although the dog cannot get up into these areas it can still search these places and will indicate the presence of an explosive very easily. The cargo bays can also be searched by placing the dog inside and completing the search within. Every aircraft is different so practice on all types to become efficient and effective. Don't let the aircraft create surprises for the handler/dog team during a call.

Let's go back to searching inside of the aircraft. Let's go through step by step, beginning with the assessment from the front of the aircraft. With the dog at a down in the gangway behind the handler, assess the front galley, making note of possible suitcases and the possibility of meals within their compartments. Then move into the aisle and assess from this position to the rear galley, making note of items left behind by passengers, closets, washrooms, overhead bins and the rear galley and storage areas as well as the rear washrooms. While the assessment is ongoing, take note of the fact that if

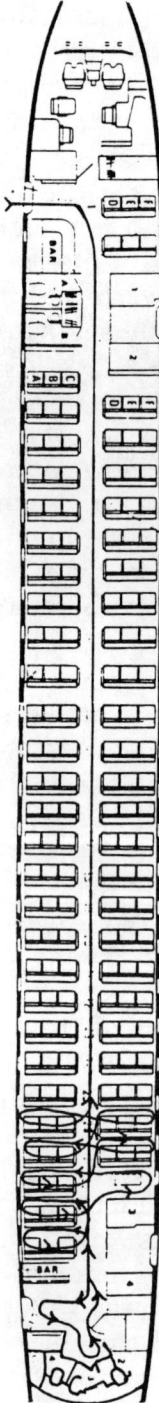

BEGIN HERE/ FRONT to REAR–CURSORY
REAR to FRONT–SYSTEMATIC

there is only one dog to search the aircraft, that the handler may have to divide the search in half. That is to say, if the aircraft is larger than a DC-9 or a 737, the search will have to be done one side at a time for the best efficiency and effectiveness. The larger aircraft, like an MD-11 or 747 or A-340, have a large seating section down the middle of the aircraft with bins overhead. Complete from the middle of the aircraft to the outer wall on one side first and then repeat the same search from the middle to the other outer wall. The process can be reversed from outer wall to the middle if the handler wishes. However, keep it the same throughout so that the handlers automatically go into the same search routine on each of the different aircraft.

With the assessment out of the way, the handler can now bring in the dog for its cursory search or scan. The cursory can begin within the front galley followed by a systematic search. There is nothing wrong with this as long as the handlers keep this system the same on all aircraft. Should the handlers choose to do a quick cursory within the front galley and then straight down the aisle to the rear galley, then this too is acceptable. Again, as the trainer, make sure that the handlers keep to this system continuously for all aircraft. This will insure that nothing is ever missed. However it is decided that the front will be done, now have the handlers do the cursory or scan down the aisle to the back galley.

Once the cursory of the rear galley is completed, finish it off with a concise systematic search. Should a hide be placed in the rear washroom, make a mental note of airflow at the rear of the aircraft. Is there a vent that is sucking the air from the center of the aircraft to the outer walls or is it the opposite direction? Whatever the direction is, make certain that it is noted by the handlers before the search begins. The reason for this is that if the flow of air is from the center to the outside wall, then there is a possibility that the dog will indicate the explosive where scent has pooled along the floor and towards the wall. Some handlers or trainers will say that this is a poorly trained dog and that it should have picked it up at the bathroom door. For one thing, the dogs will indicate and confirm wherever the scent is at its heaviest form or pooled in the greatest concentration. For another, no one knows how the scent is travelling because no one can see it. If you can see or know exactly where the scent is going, then you don't need a dog. You have just become a very rich person. Air currents push and or pull the scent in mysterious ways. This is why the dog is such an accurate tool.

With the back area completed, move into the passenger area. Begin however you have determined the search will be. For the purposes of this book, let's describe searches of two different aircraft, a DC-9 and an A-340.

● DC-9 – from the rear seats to the front seats. Assuming that all of the arm rests have been placed into an upright position beforehand (this gives the dog more room to move and allows it to sit without the distraction of something at its butt). Starting on either side first, command the dog to FIND IT, searching low between the seats first; placing its nose under the individual seats and between the cracks as well as checking the magazine pockets and small folding trays in a smooth sweeping fashion before getting onto the seats. Check to see if in fact the fabric of the seats and pockets has a low or high porosity factor by placing your mouth onto the fabric and blowing into it. On the older aircraft, your breath will easily flow through the material, which means that the scent or odor of the explosive will easily go through the material, therefore allowing the dog to detect the scent with ease. If the materials are newer, your breath will not go through and on the newer aircraft also come newer designs of seats and magazine pockets. The newer models of magazine pockets are all enclosed except for the opening at the top. If this is the case, be sure that the handlers are instructed to have their dog's nose go along the tops of these pockets so that the scent can be more readily obtained by the dog.

● With the bottoms finished, now have the dog jump onto the seats and further check the joints between the seats. Then have the dog stretch itself upward (if used to this position) to the overhead bins, or as I always suggest for the beginners, have the dog place its front paws on the seats ahead (headrests) and with the fingers, tap at the areas as follows: a) the back or rear bottom corner of the bin, b) then along to where the bin latch is and then c) along to the area where the other bottom corner meets with the bottom corner to the next overhead bin. Nothing found, go across to the other side of the aisle and repeat the process, searching on the floor between the seats, making sure the pockets are searched properly, up on the seats and up onto the headrests on the seat ahead and along the bottoms of the overhead bins. The format of the search is like that of a figure eight – the same as the buses. Then repeat across the aisle again to the next seats ahead and so on. This is a free flowing figure eight search and the dogs catch on fast.

● There are some characteristics of this search that trainers and handlers should be aware of. First, until the dogs get to find their first hide in an overhead bin, the dogs will require coaxing. They will need encouragement to stretch to those areas indicated by the handler. If a dog is having difficulties accepting the fact that it has to lift itself up to search the overhead bins, then the trainer can, before the teams get into the formal searching aspects in aircraft, make all the searches for the hides in the overhead bins. Make the first hide in the third or fourth bin (quick hides) and just have the dog go from one side to the other checking only the overhead bins until the dog(s) are confident with searching for the high hides. This always works and it will take a few seats thereafter for the dog to settle down and search along the bottoms of the seats (along the floor) first because the first thing they will do on their own is to jump upon the seats and go high. Do not worry about this, as it will work itself out. This happens on the aircraft and not the buses because the center armrests usually hinder the dogs to the point where they are bothered by the armrest around their feet, some more than others. So make the search easier for the dog and the handler. Remember that we want the learning to be done in such a manner that training doesn't become a downer for everyone involved.

● Second, if the dog does not want to reach up, trainers will often see the handlers try to physically make their dogs reach to the higher limits. Stop this immediately because it doesn't work. It just causes the dog to avoid the whole situation as soon as the handler gets close to the dog. The dog just shuts down because it thinks that its handler is about to bear-hug it and lift it upward, or is about to grab onto its paws and front legs and lift it higher. The dogs have to want to do it on their own so use the method described.

● Third, once the dogs get the hang of the high searches, you will begin to observe the dogs stretching on their own towards the overhead bins, checking the joints as indicated by the handler. They just learn to enjoy the search because they

know eventually that there something in it for them. Never ever lose hope. Patience is a priceless gift for training.

● Continue on until the front of the aircraft is reached. Never be afraid to push the dogs. Some handlers and or trainers say that a 20-minute search is the maximum for the dog to search and that it should have a find at the end of the 20 minutes and get its reward. Wrong! It is better to push the dog to become mentally and physically stronger for the searches. Have each dog do a complete search for one hide aboard the aircraft, because it will have to in a real situation. However, not only does the dog become mentally stronger, so does the handler. This is, believe it or not, mentally hard work. Mix the size of the search areas for each dog. Although some agencies require for testing purposes that the dogs have to search for a minimum of 30 minutes, I find that it is not totally neces-sary. What I found through my observations was that most of the dogs were more than capable of maintaining an hour-long search, especially if they were exercised properly every day and did not become bored if a hide was not found within that hour's time. We sometimes do not want to give the dogs the credit that is due to them. If the team is a happy team, then work becomes an enjoyable event.

- To get the dogs into these smooth flowing figure-eights, set out two hides per aircraft, one low among the seats or in the galleys and one high inside of the overhead bins. This will create a good establishment of search ethics for the dog. The repetitions within each of the venues will teach the dog to search efficiently and effectively in each of them.

  A-340 – searching this aircraft should be no different than searching a DC-9. The system is the same. However, there is a difference in the amount of area that has to be searched. Just take the DC-9, stretch it way longer and cut it in half long ways down the middle and add a middle row of seats five to six wide. It is just a larger aircraft with a lot more seats.

- As with the DC-9, the handlers have the option to cursory search the front galley and then the aisles, or cursory search and systematically search the front galley then cursory search the aisle to the rear. It is whatever the team likes to do best,

as long as it is done in the same manner consistently for all aircraft.

● Now cursory search (or scan the aisle left or right side first) to the rear of the aircraft. Cursory search the rear galley and then complete a systematic search of the same. Now move into the passenger area. Your middle row will be approximately five seats wide while on either side along the walls the seats will be two and three wide. There are a lot of seats. There will be a row of overhead bins along the outer walls and there will be two rows of overhead bins over top the middle row of seats, each parallel with the two aisles.

● When the searches begin in the passenger area, divide the inside of the passenger area in half, otherwise it will become too much for the handler to observe his/her dog, as it is too difficult to just move across with the dog because of the middle seats. As the team begins along the outer wall, it searches in the same manner, low along the floor, onto the seats, onto the headrests of the seat ahead, then to the overhead bins. Then down and across to the other side.

● With the middle row start the dog as usual, between the seats low along the floor with the dog's nose under the seats, into the cracks between the seats as well as the magazine pockets. The difference here is that the dog will only go two or three seats in and then the handler will direct the dog onto the seats; again, commanding it to check out the cracks between the seats all along until it comes to the aisle at which time the handler will get the dog up onto the headrest and up to the overhead bins. Continue this system down the aisle until the team reaches the front. Then go back to the rear of the aircraft to complete the other side. Going to the rear of the aircraft again ensures that the same system of search is consistent so nothing can be missed

Once your teams are confident and working well as teams, be sure to include the members or security personnel who work the EVDs in the training scenarios. As a trainer, observe their actions so as to always be there to assist them with their mistakes so they too can become efficient and effective. This is always about teamwork and these people are most likely to be there first unless the detector dog teams are stationed at the air terminal. One very important issue with regards to the EVD operators: I have always made it a habit of not training with NG BASED explosives in the air terminals, cargo sheds at the terminals and aboard aircraft. I have actually made it a habit to not use TNT BASED sticks in the same areas because of the heavy molecular make-up of these explosives. The molecules of these explosives tend to stay in the air for long periods of time (sometimes days) and it can wreak havoc with the EVDs, thus creating false situations.

I am sure that you must think that I am not a great fan of hi-tech machines. That is not entirely true. What I am not a fan of are the untruths about how well these machines work when it has been proven over and over again that they very unreliable by themselves and should never be trusted by themselves. I dislike the untruths that are being said of these machines at the expense of the reliably proven dog detector teams. Together, I believe you have a 100% success rate. The dogs by themselves are very high in this category and if the course-training standard is of a high quality and the teams keep up with their maintenance training, I believe a 99.99% success rate is very possible. I dislike it especially when regulators in our country's capital wish only to support the hi-tech end for the security of our air terminals. I dislike the fact that our regulators feel these hi-tech machines are totally enough because this is Canada and nothing ever really happens in this country. I dislike this because it brags of a false sense of security for our carriers and our flying passengers.

5) Buried Hides

Buried hides are self-explanatory. It seems to be the least used aspect of explosive detection because there is rarely the need to locate buried explosives from the criminal end of things. There are only a handful of calls that I can recall where the dog was required to locate buried explosives. However, it should be taught because no matter how few the calls, there will be that certain day where the dog will be required to search for the buried explosive.

In most cases, the dog will be off line and searching a large open area as it would if an article search was in progress. This is not about landmines and booby traps. This is relatively easy to train for and can be done at the end of the course. The explosives should be buried at the start of the course. A site that is safe from strangers coming in and removing the hides should be found. The hide, which can be up to five pounds, should be in a sealed container and then buried three to four inches under the ground and just left there until the end of the course. Other holes of the same size should be dug out and refilled to simulate other possible hides and to insure that the dog is not keying on the disturbed ground. Although the dogs will key on and investigate fresh and old disturbances, the dog should not be totally intrigued by them and should only investigate. The hole with the hide should interest the dog and it should be willing to take a deep sniff of the ground and then sit to confirm. The dog should not scratch or dig at the hide. This is a no-no.

When setting up for this part of the scenario training, choose an area where explosives can be buried slightly under the surface (two inches) and under rubble such as lumber or rocks. For the buried hides that will be scattered throughout, two variations can be used; a hole for the hide that will be filled in with loose dirt and a hole for the hide that will be refilled with dirt only to the top of the hide and then covered with the original grass plug. Be sure that there are several neutral holes throughout the area. The use of freshly dug holes for your hides should be discouraged. What will happen here is that the dog will become accustomed to finding a hide within the fresh hole and will, upon locating one, expect to find something there and if it doesn't, it will start to dig at the spot trying to find the hide.

Begin practicing on easy, shallow hides. Choose a squared off area that contains several cuts into the ground (all previously done days before) and one small shallow hide. Send the dog out to FIND IT, directing it from side to side of the search area and into the wind. As soon as it indicates the hide (REMEMBER WHERE IT IS!) be prepared to command the dog to SIT as soon as its nose is in the hide and it appears that the dog may scratch or dig at it. Timing is everything.

Vary the age of the hides. Vary the size of the hides. Some of the hides need not just be a few sticks of explosive. Some of the hides should be 20 to 30 sticks of explosive placed inside of a green garbage bag and then buried in a shallow hole and left to soak for six hours, one day, another for two days and another for three days. Some can be buried near or in the bush, some in the open fields and some near a marshy area. Again, it is practice, practice and practice.

Search Training Rules and On-Scene Conduct

Every trainer should stress to the new trainees that there are rules of conduct to be followed for everyone's safety. There are rules of conduct for training and there are rules of conduct for calls. These are above and beyond the regular policies and procedures that your department already has.

Search Training Rules

a) Wherever possible, use only explosives for training your teams. Try hard not to fall for the pseudo-explosives that come in marker pens. These are not as accurate as explosives and tend to make all of us lazy trainers. Remember, in order to make the teams as efficient and effective as possible, the trainer must be able to think like a terrorist and/or a bomber to make the scenarios wrapped in realism. This cannot be accomplished by making little marks on the outsides of vehicles, luggage and desks. These pseudo-explosives do not get the dogs to work for the scent. Also, when was the last time you heard of a terrorist or bomber who used pseudo-explosives to blow up a vehicle? Then why would you want to use pseudo-explosive for training?

b) Always use a number one and number two-man system during training. If number one man sets out the hides, the exact location and the type of explosive with the weight should be marked in the handler's notebook. When all of the training is over, number one man will give his/her notebook to number two man, turning to the page that indicates where all of the explosives are. Number two man will then call out each location of a hide, making note of the weights; i.e., two sticks

127

or one pound of geogel . . . As each location is cleared, that particular location should be ticked off and so on with the next hides after that. Initial and return to the number one handler. Once all the hides are set out, never leave the area. Always have someone watch the hides.

c) Always, always carry or transport explosives in government approved magazines while travelling from one location to the next.

d) Carry all explosives to be used for training in a metal ammo box that has an airtight lid to it.

e) Never have the heavy explosives (TNT and NGs) stored together in one magazine. The explosives will become cross-contaminated.

f) For health reasons, always handle explosives with surgical gloves. Be careful of your skin coming into contact with them or being confined in a small room where there is poor ventilation when using Nitro Based explosives. Otherwise, severe headaches or nausea may set in, as well as rapid heartbeats will occur. When you are through using the gloves, never dispose of them in the area the training is being done. You will forget and while the dog is doing its search, it will come across them at the most inopportune time and sit to confirm a find. Either have the trainer put them into his/her pocket or get rid of them away from the area.

g) When training at an air terminal have your department design and make a training ledger sheet like the following. This sheet or likeness thereof can be kept with your records as well as left with the person in charge of airport security for their records. It helps everyone keep tabs on training done and in what areas the hides were. This will give other EVD operators information on the training should one of their EVDs give a positive reading and nothing is found.

TRAINING MEMO

agency training: _____ date/time started: _____

type of training: _____ authority notified: _____

type and weight of explosive used: _____

_____

_____

_____

EDD members: reg# _____ reg # _____ reg # _____

venue used: 1) aircraft 2) cargo sheds 3) air terminal

location of hide(s): _____

_____

_____

_____

EVD members: reg #_____ reg # _____ reg # _____

date/time completed: _____

comments: _____

_____

_____

_____

signed/reg.#:_____

h) Training on aircraft should have its own training memo that can be left with the flight crew. I know there have been a few incidents where passengers have found explosives on the aircraft as it was reaching altitude. This is very frightening for the passengers and can give reason for litigation when this happens. Not only that, but it is important to keep good relations between the airlines that offer their equipment for training and the police departments involved. The way to accomplish this is to have a failsafe initiated between the trainers and the flight crews. The easiest way to do this is to have a training ledger for aircraft that can be placed with the flight log. When the crews come back on board, they will find this training ledger attached to their log giving the captain information on what explosive was used, where it was hidden and what department and officers were involved. The captain can then check these areas to be sure that nothing was left behind. Should something be found, it can be determined right then and there if the explosive is that of the training members or if it is there as a result of a crime. Either way, the appropriate action can be taken.

TRAINING MEMO - AIRCRAFT

AGENCY TRAINING: _____

DATE/TIME STARTED: _____

TYPE: EXPLOSIVES _____

_____

NARCOTICS _____

AUTHORITY NOTIFIED: _____

_____

GATE: _____

TYPE OF AIRCRAFT: _____

AIRLINE COMPANY: _____

LOCATION of HIDE(S): _____

_____

_____

_____

MEMBERS INVOLVED: reg # _____

reg # _____

reg # _____

DATE/TIME COMPLETED: _____

COMMENTS: _____

_____

_____

_____

SIGNED: reg # _____

The above format can be made to fit a small sheet of paper (4 x 6 inches) or a POST-IT pad with the adhesive on the back for easy placement onto the log so the memo won't be lost.

i) Always notify ahead of time the people most likely to be in charge of an area where you plan to do the training.

j) Be sure that your soak times are long enough for the venue used.

k) Always be aware of air currents.

l) When placing out the hides, be sure that the dogs cannot get at them and that they are not placed next to an electrical or heat source.

m) Be sure that the handlers are equipped with their dogs' reward toy before the training sessions start.

n) Always advise your trainees that when you talk to them while they are conducting a search with their dogs, they are never to take their eyes off of their dogs. The handlers can converse and work at the same time without any problems at all.

Call Conduct (On Scene)

By time the team is called out and is arriving at the scene, you can be assured that there are still going to be a whole lot of people there and that the complainant(s) has been asked a lot of questions at least twice. Prepare yourself for such a situation. No matter how disorganized the area is, keep a cool head. Civilians, for one, have no idea what is going on or what they should be doing. The police personnel, on the other hand, have been told numerous times what is expected of them and I guarantee that you will still have to remind them what they should be doing to help the detection team out. Whether the team is on a search warrant or on a bomb threat call, there are some pertinent questions the team can ask.

Search Warrants

a) What areas have already been searched?

This is important to know what areas were done and who completed the searches. You will want to ask these people what they observed and if anything in the areas searched looked out of place or was moved.

b) Has any evidence been located and if so, was it moved at all? Where was it located and where is it now ?

You will want to know this information. It may give you a clue to the bomber himself. It may also tell you about what you are looking for and where.

c) What type of explosive is expected to be found?

Once again this is pertinent information. What you are looking for and perhaps how much will help you to decide how fine or systematic you will have to work your dog or if you will work your dog really loose, i.e., are you looking for something with a heavy and strong odor like an NG or is it something like an emulsion, which has a very subtle odor to it?

d) In what areas is the searching being concentrated?

In what area(s) is the search to be done and why is very important to know so a plan can be devised. If you are in an area where there are a lot of rooms, for example, ask the investigators where and why they are concentrating in those areas. Then search them first, clearing them of any suspicions. However, if anything is located, tell the investigators, and have them secure the area in such a way that the room with the explosives will not impede your dog's search and investigators will not be getting in your way. Complete the search of the remaining area.

e) Are there any animals such as pets or watchdogs in the immediate area?

Important to know, because if there are small pets like mice or hamsters, there is a good chance that the dog will get them and cause some grief for your department in the future. If there is a watchdog such as a pitbull, you as a handler do not need the grief of having a dogfight that could end your dog's life or have him put out of commission for a long time.

f) Any civilians in the search area?

This is especially important if you have a dual-purpose dog (street/explosive). It is possible that the handler and his dog may startle a person just enough that the person's reactions may cause the dog to react aggressively towards them. Also, if these people are the suspects, they do not need to see the handler and the dog working. It is best to get everyone out.

g) Are there any police personnel still in the search area?

If there are, get everyone out unless they can do something in another area altogether away from the immediate search area. When the handler comes around with the dog to work, I guarantee that the police personnel will not be working but rather watching the dog doing the search.

h) Anything that is found or confirmed and is behind a locked or closed cupboard, immediately advise the investigators that they are to contact the bomb techs to care for this particular find. It is imperative to call in the experts for something like this for safety reasons.

Bomb Threats

Suggested questions prior to detector dog search.

a) What is the area to be searched? Is it a factory, a house, a vehicle? Knowing what the area to be searched is very important. Know what is inside, such as caustic chemicals that could harm you or your dog. Is the area to be searched sound? How big is the area?

b) Is the person who made the threats known? Is it a known group or organization? Are there pictures available of the person(s)? It is sometimes a strange twist of fate that this person could still be in the building and the team just may run into the accused without knowing what they look like.

c) Has this person done this before? What were the results? It could be that this person has done this before and in a peculiar manner or in a peculiar place. Or perhaps this person has been a frequent guest at your local padded cell motel up on the hill.

d) If this is the work of a group, what is their goal? Is this a personal grudge of a jilted lover or a recently ugly divorce? Is it an environmentalist group or anti-abortionist group? Then you could look for vehicles nearby to search or gas rooms of buildings.

e) Was there any mention of the type of explosive to be used? Any information of this nature will help the team decide how the scene will be searched. For example, if it is NG base then the search will start with a scan or a cursory throughout the area because it is easy for the dog to locate. However, the information has to be really sound.

f) Is there any mention of time the explosive device is set to go off?

If there is a time and it is like ten hours away, then begin the search in the areas that could cause disruptions, i.e., gas or electrical rooms. If the device is supposed to go off within the next 30 minutes to one hour, then wait for the time to pass by (even if it means the bomb blows) and then do the search. Discretion is yours to use.

g) Are there still civilians in the search area? Do not begin your search until they are all out. The team does not need any unnecessary distractions during the search.

h) Has a search been attempted? How much of the area was searched?

i) How old is this call?

j) Are police personnel still inside? Advise them (not by radio) that the search is about to begin.

These are little things that a handler can do to help make the search more efficient. Do not just get the information from an investigating officer and then start the search. Be wise. Ask for the complainant and ask him or her directly any questions that pertain to the call even though the officer asked several questions already. Sometimes they forget to ask that all-important question because so much is going on all around them.

Arson and Tactical Unit Assistance

Probably the hardest work a handler will ever have to do is trying to convince the arson unit, which investigates all explosions, and the tactical unit, which the bomb techs are part of, the value of using the dogs at all bomb calls and post blast situations. It is frustrating, to say the least, when you are part of a specialized unit that performs what no else can and yet there is always a void between you and the other specialists. It seems that the handler/dog teams are always having to prove themselves capable to the others and that they too are part of the crime fighting brotherhood.

Do not worry about it too much. It seems that wherever there is a dog unit with specialized teams in it, par for the course is always having to tell these people that we are here to help and that we can do the work. We as part of the whole team can make their work a lot simpler and easier; but not without proving yourself first. Why? Because that's the way it is until management opens their own eyes to the problem first. Do not give up. There are always a few good people within these other units who are willing to give the unit a chance and are grateful for any service that the handler/dog team may provide.

In the U.S., there seems to be greater respect for the handler/dog teams, whether or not they are specialists or regular patrol teams, than there is in Canada. There is so much kingdom building within the ranks of our managers that any sort of assistance or expert help is classified as an intrusion into their realm. Sharing the glory is out of the question.

However, there are things that, as a trainer, you can do to build up a rapport with these other units. First, make sure that your handler/dog teams take part with the tactical unit whenever they put on PETA courses (police explosives technician assistant). Become part of the team by getting involved. As a matter of fact, all who take my course have to have taken the PETA course before they can take the EDD course. Once you have taken this course two or three times, then the handlers can go about setting up demos with the tactical unit to show them what the dog is capable of. By this time they are usually glad that the handlers are doing these demos for them.

As for the arson units, get involved with them too. Take part in the post-blast courses they put on in conjunction with the tactical units. Learn from the arson investigators what it is they would like to see the handler/dog teams do for them. Make a list and then act upon it. Set out to work with your handlers and their dogs to make the requests of the arson unit viable. Make them want to include your teams because of the good work they are doing, not because they have to. It is an ongoing process that can show rewards sometime down the road.

Certification & Problem Solving

Course Certification Requirements

All that is required for Transport Canada approval, Federal Aviation Agency approval or approval of any police department in North America, is included in the DDSI Course Training Standard Manual.

All of the first bases are covered or learned and all that is left for any department is to create their own Course Examination/Re-Validation Tests. Throughout North America and Europe, so much kingdom building goes on regarding standards. The U.S., for example, is basically torn into three major sections; the East, the Mid-West and the West. In Canada, there is the RCMP, the OPP (Ontario Provincial Police), there is the East or Toronto area and there is the West. In Europe, Germany plays the biggest role, but there is France and Belgium too. The *Landespolizeischule fur Diensthundfuhrer* in Stukenbrock, West Germany, perhaps plays the biggest role world wide when it comes to setting standards for police departments. Theirs is a basic standard that covers all aspects of police work and it is easy to train by their methods. However, a lot of departments have really complicated their system, turning it into something too technical for most handlers and dogs from something that is, shall I say, pure and simple.

Throughout the system that I have put together, I demand simplicity and I demand that all handlers are helped throughout the course. I also give the trainers options, no dead end streets, but choice routes from which the TEAM can grow.

Of all the standards that are out there for the various police departments to choose from, which standard is the best? Who has the best standard that covers everything that a police department requires? I am not sure if one exists. I have studied many course standards and overall, the one standard that stands out the best is that of the Royal Canadian Mounted Police. It covers everything that they require of their officers and dogs to function as a federal police force. I like a lot of what they have, but there are a few things that I would not use for my training course. The same is true of the Lackland Airforce Base Dog Training Standard. There are a lot of things that I like about their system too, but I only use about one percent of what they teach. It is not because I think they are not good; quite the contrary, I think they are very good, but that one percent is all I require for my system.

As far as trainers go, who decides who will be a trainer? Who decides which standard is the best? Which one stands up in court the best? Any one Course Training Standard will. What determines the outcome of the majority of court cases is not the standard itself, but what the standard teaches or perhaps doesn't teach. In most court cases I have read of or experienced myself, the expert witness testimony covers the course-training standard rather quickly but well. Documentation, on the other hand, is covered extremely thoroughly. If the teams are to have anything ready for court at all, it had better be good and concise training records and records of all calls attended where the dog was used. This is the way defence lawyers like to attack the handlers' and departments' credibility. These training records are more important than life itself, so to speak. You can be a successful self-taught handler with nothing to indicate to the defence lawyers that you've taken an accredited course that makes you an expert witness. But show up to court with a resume as thick as a phone book and training records to accompany the resume – the handler is golden. Documenting all training, all calls, all successes and failures (explain why there were failures, as most are generic in structure – usually handler error or scent disturbance).

Whichever standard you choose, just be sure that the maintenance training is regular and challenging and that everything is documented.

We have chosen the standard that fits departmental needs and we know that documentation is extremely important. Another important aspect to the course certification requirements is the Course Examination/Re-Validation Test Scenarios. How are you going to ensure that the teams are competent and certified to carry on with the work of making sure that the flying public and the airline companies are safe from explosives? There is only one way to accomplish this and that is to create a system of evaluation that permits the trainer to observe the handler and the dog complete a search for explosives in each of the six different areas or venues.

Each venue is an aspect of police work when a team is on an actual call. These six venues are: 1) Vehicle Search, 2) Rooms, 3) Lockers, 4) Aircraft, 5) Cargo, 6) Luggage.

The buried hides' test I leave out of the certifications and re-certifications, but complete it towards the end of the course training. The reason for this is because if your re-certification ends up being in December or January, the ground up here in Canada becomes very frozen and it is impossible to work under those conditions. Any other part of the certifications can be completed indoors. Therefore, I make buried hides a monthly training situation while the ground is good. If you do make it part of the certification, be sure all certifying is done in the summer months consistently. The certification tests should always be completed all at once to ensure quality control of the certified team. If you leave one aspect of the testing out until later on in the year, then you do not have a certified team until that aspect has been completed. Now let's go through each aspect of the certification in detail.

1. Vehicle Search (Two Hides)

A minimum of ten vehicles (cars and/or trucks) will be required per hide. Vehicles used for this part of the certification test should be frequently used. The setting can either be inside of a garage or at an out-of-doors car lot. However, it must be noted that whatever the area to be used, it should be large enough to accommodate 20 vehicles or more.

There will be two hides of explosives; one inside of the vehicle and one on the outside of the vehicle. Each hide will be in a separate vehicle far apart from each other. Each hide will be made up of a different explosive and weigh approximately 1/2 pound to 2 pounds.

Each hide will be aged for at least one hour.

Note: as per this course, the exterior of a vehicle will be designated as any area on the outside of the car, including the engine area. The trunk area will be deemed part of the interior.

2. Rooms (Two Hides)

For this scenario, it is preferred that the test site be uncleaned or used motel rooms. However, the use of a firehall (has living quarters) would be acceptable.

Five rooms will be required for this part of the certification test. Once again, two different explosives will be utilized, one for each of the hides. Each hide will be aged for at least 1/2 hour.

3. Lockers (One Hide)

This scenario can be completed in any area that has many commonly used lockers. These areas can include shopping malls, YMCA and bus depots.

For the purposes of a realistic test, the lockers should contain recently worn clothing. The hide will be aged for at least 1/2 hour. If possible, be sure there are a minimum of 50 lockers for the teams to search.

4. Aircraft (Two Hides)

This scenario requires the team to search a groomed or ungroomed aircraft and locate two hidden explosives (alleged devices). In this test the hides can be of the same explosive. However, it will be left up to the discretion of the instructor whether or not the hides will be of two different types of explosive. Areas to be searched will be the washrooms, all seats and overhead bins and galleys. The hides will be aged for at least 1/2 hour.

The trainer can add the third hide outside of the aircraft and may wish to include it as part of the test. This will be his/her option and it can only add to the credibility of the team being tested. If so, the teams will search all cargo holds and landing gear receptacles.

Note: Due to the molecular density of certain explosives, it is recommended that TNT and NG based explosives not be used for training and testing purposes on aircraft.

5. Cargo (1 Hide) – Air Terminal Sheds

For this test scenario, the explosive hide will be concealed in packaging similar to cargo found in the cargo area to be searched. The hide will be situated as to blend in with the other cargo. Try to incorporate as much of the cargo shed for the search so there is at least 30 minutes of search time for the team to cover. The scene should be aged for a minimum of 1/2 hour.

6. Luggage (2 Hides) – Air Terminal

In this scenario, a minimum of 30 to 40 pieces of assorted luggage will be lined up in a row (this should be done by the handler to display his/her abilities in doing an effective, efficient and safe search). This can be done in the arrivals/departure baggage loading docks at the air terminal or at the cargo shed.

This portion of the test can also be done outdoors if so desired. The luggage should all contain clothing while one suitcase will contain some food as a distraction. The trainer can also have all of the luggage placed onto a moving belt if so desired and can increase the number of bags to be searched for the test. However, the main focus here is to evaluate the dog and handler on how the dog reacts to the hide in the bag amongst the other bags; and how the handler reacts to the dog when it searches all of the luggage and comes across the food and then comes across the hide. Speed and numbers of bags searched in one hour tests, if so desired, should be done on training days during the work week.

The second search will be conducted in the seating areas of the departure lounges at the air terminal. Another handbag or briefcase will be left in the area for the team to locate. There will be an area large enough so that the team will be searching for at least 30 minutes. Each hide should be of two different explosives. These hides will be aged a minimum of 1 hour.

These scenarios can all be changed to suit the trainer's or unit's needs. This is a very user friendly system of testing and it demonstrates the capabilities of the handler and the dog: the team. Remember that as trainers the most important factor here is to certify the teams for duty. Do not get technical. Use the KISS system and you won't ever go wrong.

Course Certification/Re-Certification Rating Guide

We have just tested the teams as a whole or a unit, but we also have to evaluate the handler on his/her own abilities and the dogs' abilities. In order to rate them we have to give a mark. For departmental use, the only thing the handlers' remarks should say is either PASS or FAIL. However, as the trainer, you have to be able to come to that conclusion with a marking system. This is for the trainer's eyes only and is essential should a handlers' or dogs' credibility come into question in a lawsuit or criminal matter. The rating system is really a search conduct of the team and they are rated from EXCELLENT for a maximum of 5 points to POOR for a minimum of 1 point.

Search Conduct of the Team

EXCELLENT (5 points) search is thorough, smooth and extremely efficient.

GOOD (4 points) search is thorough and quick, but the search pattern could be more organized. Dog has breaks in concentration and needs some minor encouragement.

FAIR (3 points) search completed with difficulty, dog frequently distracted. Needs strong encouragement from the handler and the search pattern is awkward.

POOR (1 point) search completed with extreme difficulty. The dog is easily distracted and lacks motivation. The search pattern is confused.

Conduct of Dog After Alert

EXCELLENT (5 points) dog alerts on scent of explosive, works quickly to the source, confidently and unhesitatingly confirms the find using the correct trained response. No encouragement from the handler required after the initial alert.

GOOD (4 points) same general response as above but with moderate encouragement needed from the handler.

FAIR (3 points) dog alert but appears unsure, needs encouragement from the handler to confirm. Confirmation response is slow or weak.

POOR   (1 point) hard to distinguish between general interest and confirmation response. Alert is weak and the dog needs constant encouragement to confirm.

There are 10 hides to be found and 10 points for which the team is rated, with a possible total of 20 points. Team efficiency is then rated out of a possible 100 points (10 plus 10 x 5).

Problem Solving

One of the very many things courses and/or instructors try to do with all handlers is to make them into handlers <u>and</u> trainers. This is so very wrong. Handlers that are just beginning or have less than five years of dog handling experience (the operative phrase here is dog handling, not dog training) have a million things on their minds relating to understanding what their dogs are telling them, what their dogs' search personalities are and dealing with everything else that is required of them as police officers. Of all the courses that a police officer can take throughout his career and of all the positions that they can hold, nothing is more demanding mentally and physically that that of the dog handler. What trainers and courses should explicitly offer these handlers is how to become a <u>handler</u> instead of trying to turn them into handler/trainers. We should not be training these handlers about all dogs. We should be teaching them how to work with <u>their</u> dog. No handler should become a trainer unless he/she has handled more than two dogs in their tenure and should have more than five years of dog handling experience on the street.

What you are about to read in this segment has already been covered. I have been putting in little bits and pieces of information relating to the beginnings of problems. As the trainer, you are in a rather unique position to observe the little things that dogs and handlers do. These are what I call generic tendencies, or the little habits humans and dogs acquire that can become liabilities. It is very easy for us to stand back and observe and then criticize, especially when the trainer knows where all the hides are. But, the trainer is GOD and HE sees all. What the trainer observes is not to be taken as criticism.

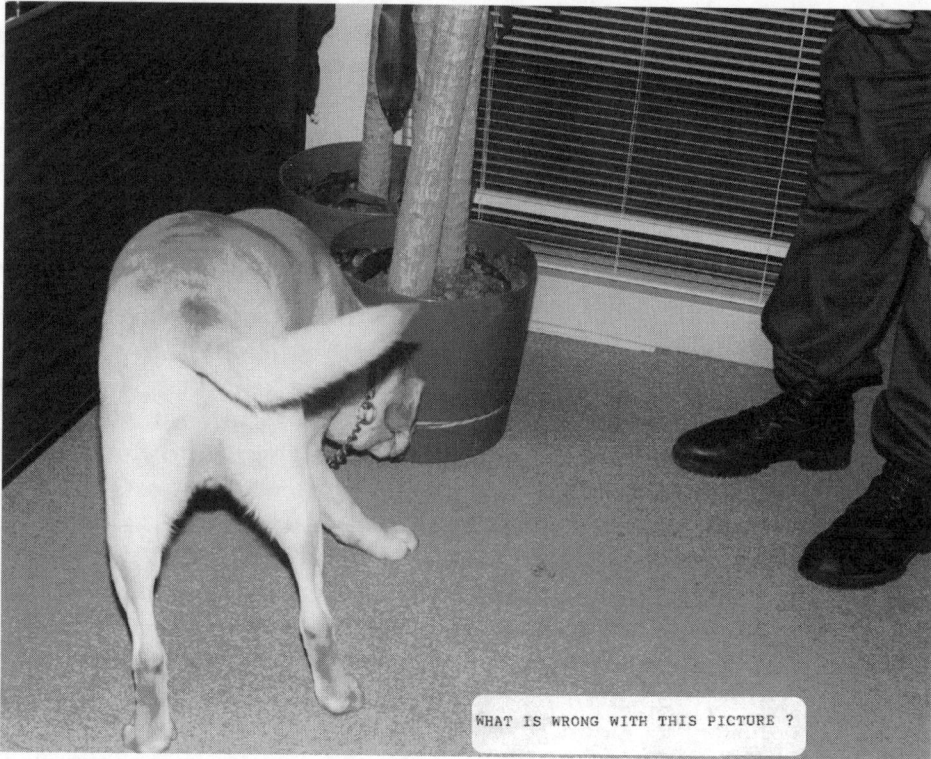

WHAT IS WRONG WITH THIS PICTURE ?

What is wrong with this picture? The dog is wearing a fairly loose metal collar, which could conceivably get hooked on something as it searches, or spark off something (not something you want happening near a bomb). The handler is also standing fairly close to the dog, which could make it difficult for him to observe the dog's reactions, especially if it goes sniffing behind the plants or the desk.

In fact, every mistake a handler makes in front of me as I observe, I relish. With my system, a mistake is never a mistake. Handlers do not have failures; they have learning experiences. Their mistakes are their teachers. As I stated earlier on in this book, I deplore trainers who stand back and let handlers fail. These are all grown men and women, who carry guns on their hips, who make decisions every day that have profound effects on those people and their lives. Then we get these same officers in as dog handlers and treat them as if they were children. This is not the way to learn and it is definitely not the way to teach to obtain the best results. The team is the equation and that is how I teach. Trainers must teach the handler and the dog as a team, not as separate entities. Why? Because the dog does not search alone; the dog completes the search under the guidance of its handler. Otherwise, we wouldn't need the handler.

From the very first day while the teams take their very first steps, I am observing those little insignificant things. Problem solving is more about preventing than it is about curing. If you have to stop to make the time to cure a problem, you are usually too late. Problem solving is not just about fixing a problem dog, it is also about fixing handler problems, such as sloppy search techniques and trying to remember what was searched and what was not searched. If the handler is taught to be sloppy, then the dog will be sloppy. As soon as the team is ready for the search scenarios, I want the teams to become efficient, effective and safe. The only way to accomplish this is to use proper search patterns and search speeds.

Search Patterns/Search Speed

A very important part of the search pattern depends upon the handlers seeing everything within the area to be searched that might be a hiding place for a device, and ensuring the dog is not only presented to this area but that the dog does search it. This is being efficient; however, the handler must be effective too. There can be no doubt that seeing the whole picture before the team starts helps with the overall search; but the handler must also remember detail. Without detail, the search is ineffective.

To better explain, the dog cannot relay to the handler that it has forgotten to search certain areas, and therefore go back and complete the search on its own. This is the challenge that is offered to every explosive detector dog handler.

Quite often we see the dog teams re-searching the areas that had just been cleared by the dog. In some cases it is because the handler has little faith in the dog; if so, then there is fault with the training course and/or the instructor. The course, together with the instructor, should create confident teams. The instructor must teach the handler to always remember what has not been searched.

The trainer must get the handlers to envision the search area and then categorize their thinking so as to know:

● What **direction** will the search begin?
● How much **area** is there to search?
● Do you do a **cursory** search?

● Would it be more effective to break the room into **sections** once the cursory search has been completed?

You are actually teaching the handler to problem solve the search area. The handler is now becoming efficient at assessing the area, so that he/she has the best opportunity to observe the area in great detail, while at the same time watching the dog for indications and what has not been searched.

However, we can teach all of this and still have a handler who will not realize the importance of recognizing his/her dog's indications and/or signals because they are paying so much attention to detail. This is a situation that requires problem solving. How do we go about solving this problem? As the trainer, you always know ahead of time where the hides are. You can surmise approximately where the team will be entering into the scent cone. Decide when the team is about three to four steps away from the scent cone; this is when you will notify the handler that they are coming very close to the hide and for the handler to drop the line and step back or just take a few paces beyond and observe the dog. The handler will begin to notice the dog's attitude change. The ears become erect, the tail may start to wag, the dog's mouth will close and it becomes very intent on searching a specific area. Before the dog got to the cone, it did not show any of these tendencies. As soon as the dog is finished and has its reward and oodles of praise, have the handler place the dog away from the area into a down position, gather all of the other handlers that are watching and have a question/answer session. Ask the handler what signs his/her dog was displaying before it got to the scent cone area and while it was in the scent cone area. The handler should give the same answers as above. Ask the other handlers if they observed any other tendencies. Then ask the group what was not searched. If any areas were noticed to be not searched, then advise the group that while they are watching the team searching, to remind the handler when everything else is done to finish searching the missed areas. This is because they are acting as the number two man who always assists the team. They are assisting one another by helping each handler to interpret the dog's indications. They are also assisting one another to observe their dogs at all times, while at the same time observing the search area and learning what is an indication and what is interest.

So now we have the group fixing or preventing search pattern problems that will very likely lead to other problems later on. They are all problem solving

Now we talk of search speed. The proper search speed is very important. Search speed should suit the dog. The dog should be allowed to search at its own speed so that it is comfortable with what it is doing. If the handler is moving too slow, the probability of the dog False Sitting becomes very high. If the handler is causing the dog to search too fast, the probability of the dog missing a hide is very high. Search speed is an important part of the search pattern.

The speed of search pattern is determined by several factors and can vary from situation to situation. Speed also varies from dog to dog, therefore the rule of thumb to follow on the speed of search should be to let the dog search at its own speed, as long as the dog is not running and is tending to the area and/or objects being searched. However, given time and numerous qualitative training sessions, the dog will begin to perfect its search pattern by working at its own comfortable speed and completing on its own the search patterns.

Cursory Searches or Scan

Variations to the normal speed can be affected by such things as:

● How much explosive are you searching for?

● How long has the hide or device been there?

● What type are you searching for? (for calls, there usually is intelligence as to what type of explosive is used)

● How much free flowing air is moving around the explosives?

● Has a designated time been given as to when the device may go off?

This is why the cursory search or scan is so important. It gives the team flexibility to work within a small time frame whenever needed. This an alternative to a problem.

Note: at no time should a scan or cursory search be considered adequate to completely clear any area. A detailed search must always be conducted after the cursory search.

Verbalization

Throughout this book I discuss verbally encouraging your dog whenever it is at the hide. Verbalization should only be used in the context of:

- Commanding the dog to start the search.

- Changing the tone in one's voice to chastise the dog for being distracted or being sloppy and to add excitement to the tone to help encourage the dog when it's becoming bored or tired or trying to verbally praise the dog for working the scent cone during its early stages of training.

- Verbalization should only be used during these times and for a very short, short moment. Verbalization is a very short moment for praise or scolding during the search in order to encourage or discourage.

- The handlers should be encouraged to be quiet while their dogs are searching and only verbalize when it is needed. If the handlers continuously verbalize, or what I call nagging the dog, there is a very good chance that the chattering will lead to false sitting. Therefore a trainer should always be aware of this ahead of time so as not to let this become a habit. This is what is known as a handler-induced problem, although this could be said of all problems that arise throughout training.

- A related aspect to verbalization and one which a trainer would have to deal with on a one to one level with the handler is Attitude. Attitude can play a negative role or a positive role in training. A positive attitude makes for a happy, smooth flowing team that wants to tackle anything that comes across their path.

A handler with a negative attitude is an explosion waiting to happen. Handlers who have a negative attitude will have a negative effect on their dog. The negativity travels to the dog from the handler's voice inflection and the handler's posture. Dogs can sense this and it does have a negative effect on them. This usually happens to handlers who have short tempers and to handlers who have problems accepting the fact that their dogs are not doing as well as the other dogs in the group. This may be an ego thing or it's just the way the handler is. Either way, the trainer will have to recognize this and deal with it.

Training Aid Problems

Training aids or locations used to hide the explosives can pose problems for the dog during searches if the trainer doesn't understand how airflow affects the scent cone. Some trainers believe that no matter where the hide is situated, the dog must be able to smell the odor from the front. For example, a hide that is placed in a desk drawer or in a locker; the understanding is that the dog will get the scent if it sniffs the complete front of the desk or the lockers. This is so wrong. In most situations such as these, the scent travels to the back of the desk and/or the locker and then down the wall to the floor. However, if a trainer does not accept this or is not aware of this, then a problem can arise. The problem that usually arises is that the trainer thinks there is either a problem with the dog or with the handler. Be careful here, because this is a situation where you can cause the handler to start losing faith in the dog when it is not the fault of the dog at all. That is why we teach the handlers to get their dogs to search all of the desk; along the fronts, along the sides, under the desk and at the back of the desks. Lockers too, along the fronts, the sides and the backs along the floor.

Hides in the ceiling can create confusion more for the dog than the handler and turn it off because it cannot get to the source. Hides in the ceiling can have the scent cone altered because the airflow or currents travel differently near the ceiling than they do in the rest of the room. To find out, just hold a lit match or lighter near the ceiling and watch which way the flame leans. If the trainer or handler is not aware of this situation, then they should fully expect the dog to indicate the odor in the room that is under the hide. But in reality, the dog will locate the scent of the hide in another area or room.

These are little things for the most part, but they do mean a lot in the long run. As trainers, we must always be aware for the team, because handlers tend to watch only the dog and not the changes in behavior or changes to the environment, it is extremely important to continuously help the teams become better. If you are a trainer, tell the teams:

- that they are going to run into safety hazards or that there are distractions coming up
- that a fan just came on and to watch for air currents
- that they are not working together with their dog

- that they are working too tight, too loose, too slow or too fast
- that they are searching the area more than once
- or that the dog is getting tired and therefore give it a short rest.

These are things that a really good trainer does for the team while they search.

Missing Hides

If the dog misses a hide, it is most likely because the handler missed the signal.

This happens because:

- the dog was moving too fast,
- the handler was too slow to react,
- the search pattern is too sloppy and irregular,
- or the scent was not strong enough due to a too short soak time.

When this happens, be sure the handler does not bring the dog back to the exact location. Have the handler start the dog a few feet away from the hide and then work back into or towards the hide. Remember that because the search pattern must be a direct and specific act of presenting each area to the dog as it is approached and that the handler should be ahead of the dog both mentally and physically when doing the detailed search pattern, there is a lot going through a green handler's mind. That is why the trainer should be telling the handler when the team is nearing the hide. This should always be done at the start of the course until the trainer is satisfied that the team is working well together. The handler then knows to slow him/herself down, step back and let the dog do its thing while at the same time the handler can observe the changes in the dog.

If the dog is missing hides because it is moving too fast or trying to sneak past the handler, then the trainer can give the handler a few tricks, like blocking the dog's way with the knee (press the dog hard against the wall) or have the handler quickly reverse the direction of the search and call the dog to change direction and re-command it to search the area it went by. This is all about problem prevention.

Remember, it is better to prevent problems rather than cure them.

Police Departments' Bastard Child

The stories, the complaints, the lack of recognition, surprise schedule changes, the lack of support for courses, the theft of budgets, taking vehicles away from the fleet, sub-standard equipment; the list can go on forever. These things never seem to change, yet the upper management of most major police departments are guilty of treating their dog units as if they were a bastard child. If anything can be taken away, it will be done without conscience from the dog unit. Throughout my career in the dog unit, I can honestly say that there has been only one commander who fought for the unit, treated it fairly and continuously gave credit for individual work. My other commanders for the most part were good, but none stood out or did the things for the section this commander did. Managers, for some reason, are incapable of getting involved with the dog unit, knowing exactly what they do, how they feel and what they need. I recently was helping a department train their explosives dogs and the commander stopped several times to observe while the training was ongoing. A few weeks later he stopped by again to watch the training. In front of the two handlers being trained, he asked me how the drug training was going. I quickly told him that this was explosives training. Right away another question came flying out of his mouth. He then asked me how the bomb dog training was going and how the Lab that I was training for the course was doing. I was flabbergasted. He had just watched the Lab run a training exercise – couldn't he see for himself, I wondered? The two handlers were embarrassed, to say the least.

If you are the commander of a specialized unit, I would expect that you would know about everything that is going on because most specialized units are small. I would expect that, as a commander, you would know what courses are going on and what each dog is being trained for. In this case, the commander should have shown more interest. It made it appear that this unit (1 of 3) was not important. Believe it or not, this lack of concern hurts morale. If you are a commander of a unit like a dog unit, do not come around to embarrass yourself and especially the members in front of other people. If you have nothing intelligent to say, then don't say anything at all.

I would like to comment on a few areas where commanders and administrators could improve their performance with respect to the dog unit. Unfortunately, the things that commanders are extremely famous for often demoralizes the members of the section and/or the unit. This then becomes an issue with their work, because people become less motivated when they are always treated like second-class citizens. For some unknown reason, commanders and the rest of the upper management are totally blind to the effects of this or feel that it just doesn't exist. I have often asked myself why someone would go out of their way to treat other people in this manner, especially when, of all the specialty units involved within a police department, the dog unit has the greatest success, is loved by the public, makes major contributions to investigations through arrests and finding evidence, and has a fairly high call load compared to some other specialties. The dog units of today work harder through training because there is more knowledge about dogs and their abilities, and as usual, handlers put in an enormous amount of their own time into the unit and work without compensation to them or their families. Yet, a majority of handlers are asked to do even more because of their unselfishness.

There are several immediate areas where commanders and upper management have negative effects on the unit. They are budgets, scheduling, use of the specialized units and courses. I will go over each of them, giving examples for each. These examples are pretty much generic and have effected most dog units.

Budgets

Budgets are what keep all departments of any business going. Without budgets, police departments would never exist. The only way around budgetary capital is to go private, and for a police service to go private is totally unacceptable to me. I realize that they do exist in Canada as well as in the U.S., but my feeling is that they are not the answer to better service or better protection of our public.

For the dog units, the items covered by their budgets are things like overtime, equipment, dog food and vet bills, vehicles, courses and, of course, dogs. Some of the bizarre things that I have experienced in the past relating to management's uncaring and unmovable attitudes is that the dogs of the unit would have to go without food for a week to ten days because the canine unit budget for food was gone. Now think of this, the commander had a university education and our working dogs were to go without food for this period of time. This is a manager who was in charge of a section, in charge of the members, expensive equipment and dogs. Demoralizing? I was beside myself not knowing where to turn, except for the fact that all the handlers were willing to pay out of their own pockets for the dog food. The first thing that this commander said was not "Thanks guys, I appreciate this," but "The department will not be reimbursing those members who buy the food out of pocket." Nobody even asked to be reimbursed. This is a commander who works for a department with a hundred million dollar a year budget. Who wouldn't be demoralized?

If any unit or squad has a budget, that budget should be theirs until the year's end. In most situations it is, unless your budget is the dog unit budget. For the most part, a year can go by without incident. The equipment is lasting well, the overtime is kept to a minimum and the dogs are healthy. However, a dog unit can count on the fact that every two or two and a half years, all hell will break loose and there will be a need to use every last penny to purchase new equipment, pay for some very large vet bills or to replace several dogs. When the poor sergeant goes to his budget to see how much money he/she has left to purchase those items, there is nothing left in that category. Yet, the dog unit did not spend any of that money because it wasn't required until now. So if the dog unit didn't spend it, where did it go and most of all, why wasn't the sergeant told? So the sergeant goes to the commander to find out where the money went. There is a lot of hesitating and finally the commander states that another unit needed new equipment and as a result, the money from the dog unit's budget had to be used because the money in the other unit's budget couldn't be touched because it had already designated those monies. Let's go to the other side of the room now; the sergeant needs a new dog to replace another aging dog that has seen its last days of street work. There are three more months left in the budget year, but the cupboard is bare. The canine budget is empty for purchasing dogs and whatever else is left in other areas has to remain there. The sergeant goes to the commander, explaining to him that the dog is desperately needed because the present one can no longer work. If the dog is not replaced, the handler will be without a dog for three months. Does another unit have any money that the dog unit can use? No they don't! You will just have to wait until the new budget comes in. My question to the commander was this, "Why couldn't the other units wait for their new equipment, especially when the old equipment was only two years old? Why couldn't they wait for another few months for the new budget?"

This happens all the time and it is wrong and it is totally unnecessary. Commanders and upper management continuously do these things without thinking of the consequences of their actions. As a commander, make each and every unit accountable for its own budget. Don't demoralize the unit by arbitrarily using their budget and worse yet, don't lie to them. If at the year's end there is money left over and the dog unit does not need the money, then make a decision with the leftover monies.

Courses

Most units or sections have qualities unique to them no matter where in the world they may work. As a result, they require expert training and ongoing updates from experts in their field, hence the need for courses and seminars.

These are courses that departments need in order to enhance their section's or unit's needs and abilities. This is ever so true of dog units. Dog units are specialized in their own way as it is, however, as with the tactical teams, these specialized areas have within them specialized mini-units.

The tactical teams will have members or small units within the unit who are snipers or bomb techs. With canine or the dog unit, you may have a small unit of drug detection dogs, arson dogs, body recovery dogs or explosive detection dogs. So as you can see, everyone requires expert instruction and the only way to receive this expertise is through, in most cases, out of town, out of state or province, and out of country courses.

I have been extremely fortunate to go on many courses throughout my career in the police service and I owe a lot to the Calgary Police Service. However, whereas members of the tactical unit or arson squad have had an easy time getting to go on courses, the members of the dog units seem to have to bleed before they go on any course. Much more argument has to come from the canine unit before they get to go compared to the other units. I have no problems with any unit or section that gets to attend these courses, but it doesn't have to be at the expense of the unit's blood, sweat and tears.

Commanders and upper management should without question be sending members of the dog units on these courses, especially with today's laws and easy litigation that snarls the abilities of the police in general and creates braver or smarter suspects. If there is a stigma that these courses or seminars are only a drunken good time, then the commander should obtain from all involved in the course or seminar a report listing how the newly-learned information will enhance the unit. I am sure that this will be accepted as something very positive, because it will further their chances of getting more courses to go on in the future.

Use of Specialty Units and Scheduling

If there is anything besides budgets that upper management or section commanders can screw up without trying, it is how they utilize the specialty dogs and what they will do to schedules to make things happen. This part of the chapter explains why commanders should be involved with handlers during training and on calls. If they did this, then they wouldn't make the kind of mistakes I am about to tell you about.

These are several situations that again are generic in nature with most departments. A situation arose in Canada where a government security force requested the use of two bomb dogs to sanitize a site where V.I.P.s were to have their conferences. The two dog handlers were notified and they said they would be there as long as their commander ok'd the call, as they were both on days off and would have to be paid for call-out. The tactical teams were notified of the situation and, as they were working, there wouldn't be any problems attending the call with the EDDs. At any rate, situations like this require that both units attend all explosive related calls, as it should be.

As it worked out, someone within the tactical team was not happy with the way the government security force member went about procuring the dog teams and the bomb techs for the call. Somewhere in all of this mess, the two EDD teams had their schedules changed to accommodate the two tactical teams, who all of a sudden were on call-out status, and the two EDD teams were now working. Now two tactical teams, nine members on each team, were on double time. That is, 18 members earning double-time. Originally, the only members on call-out status would have been the two EDD teams. I have to ask myself, if I were a commander running a tight ship, would I allow this incident to happen? I would have thought that budgets were a priority. To add insult to injury, one of the tactical teams decided that while the dog was working, they would lay themselves down on the chairs and lounges and watch the search. I recall that while working my dog, the tactical members would have been searching everything shoulder height and higher. This is how it should be done. After hearing this, it came as no surprise to me that these two handlers were totally disgusted with how they were treated. I was surprised they even wanted to continue being specialists.

The way EDDs are utilized at some airports is appalling. Once again, it is the commanders who decide how it will be done, and it is sometimes clear that public safety comes second to section budgets. All EDD handlers take their work very seriously. They have to go through some very serious training and are guided or governed by some very tough rules. One of the many things discussed for airports is that the safety of the passengers, airline personnel and the police and private security personnel that work there comes first. Hence, some guidelines are laid out as to how suspicious packages or suspicious luggage are handled. In Europe, for instance, anything left unattended is destroyed. The owners are given one call on the P.A. system and if no one comes to claim the item, it is placed into a container, taken away to a specific site and destroyed. In Canada, our security personnel, be it police or private, look at the item and, while the public is walking all around them within a few feet, they open it up to see what is inside. We Canadians are so nice and considerate. One day, an airport authority and a city police department are going to have such a big class action suit against them that they won't know which way to turn.

In one city, a briefcase was left by itself, and whether or not it was related to a bomb threat is not important. The police in this particular situation put the briefcase onto a luggage cart and wheeled it to the information booth where people were working and passengers were walking by. They taped an area 50 feet by 50 feet off and wouldn't let anyone enter the area. This was good, but instead of keeping them away from the area, they let them watch. Not a good plan. Then the EVD operator came in with his little expensive machine, placed a probe on it, and then proceeded to try and get the probe inside to get a sample of air. Now, I don't know what the manufacturers of these EVDs taught these operators, but one of the things I learned from the bomb techs is not to move the item at all if possible. Well here was a guy who might as well have opened it. Next came the handler with his dog, who began his search away from the case and worked his way towards it. At least he was doing something right. Nothing was found. But the point here is, this is what handlers have to deal with. That case should have been taken to a designated safe area of the air terminal and taken care of there.

In another situation, airport police found a suspicious tool kit. Bomb techs were requested. They refused to come out and, believe it or not, contrary to training, they told the police officer involved to open it and see what was in there because it probably wasn't anything to worry about. This officer refused and requested a dog handler to come out. The handler came out, got all the information from the investigating officer, looked at the tool kit and called the sergeant of the bomb squad and explained the situation, also telling them they should come out. The answer was no. The handler was told to take care of the situation. The handler was told to use his dog and if the dog didn't indicate or confirm, then he was to open the tool kit himself. The commander of the section agreed.

Another situation happened not too long ago and again included the tactical unit and the commander. A robbery took place at one bank, where the culprit made a phone call to the teller of the bank, telling her to place a certain amount of money into a bag and then place it into a car parked across the street. She was then instructed not to call the police for a period of time, otherwise he would blow up the bank she worked in as well as a few of the other branches throughout the city. The explosives were already in place. She followed the directions to a tee.

The tactical team/bomb squad was put on call-out status due to the mention of explosives. They searched that particular bank by hand all day and, while they did think of the EDDs, they did nothing to request the presence of the dog. The EDD team was available. Had they called the EDD team out, the search would have been done in a matter of an hour or two and saved the commander a lot of money. Here is blatant ignorance on the commander's part. The department spent a lot of money to train the EDD teams just to sit around. Like most handlers, they want to be involved. They want to be able to help. Most of all, they all want to do what they were trained for. Most of the handlers I have come to know are extremely professional and highly motivated, key ingredients for great handlers, but unfortunately these ingredients are no longer recognized by commanders.

I hate dumping on commanders and upper management in this manner, but these people destroy the will and heart of a unit that makes them look good. Police work is not just about community-based policing. Police work is not just about the tax-paying public. It is about the men and women who are out on the front lines serving our taxpayers while the commanders and upper managers are too busy pretending to be politicians. Handlers do try to speak out, but unfortunately the reprisals are not worth it for them. It is actually easier to face a bullet than it is to sit down and reason with commanders and upper management. I am no longer with the police department, yet no matter where I travel in North America or elsewhere in the world, the stories are relatively the same.

These are all things that demoralize not only individual members, but demoralize whole units. Working in a dog unit is the most dangerous aspect of police work today. It is all front line work and working while in a demoralized state is dangerous to all handlers. I would go so far as to say that it is also dangerous to the public.

There needs to be a new breed of commanders and upper management who are taught better management and people skills in order to get the most and the best out of their people without demoralizing them. I know this happens with dog units everywhere. I know it is wrong and it is totally unnecessary. <u>But so do the commanders and upper managers.</u>

Explosives

Although 99.99% of dog handlers are not bomb techs, there are the chosen few who are both tech and handler. These people have a vast knowledge of devices, explosives and have the ability to render safe any explosive device. This combination is probably more frequent in the U.S. than Canada. However, all EDD handlers must know about explosives. An EDD handler should be able to identify any commercial and military explosive and be able to tell anyone what the base is of that particular explosive.

I have always told any EDD handler that I have trained to:

- Know your explosives.
- Know what their content is.
- Know what kind of shelf life each different explosive has.
- Know what their sensitivity is.
- Know if that particular explosive is still being manufactured and where.
- Know who to contact for information on military and commercial explosives.
- Know who to contact in the commercial industry who can supply your unit with explosives, information on new explosives and how to set up an arrangement to obtain new explosives, and
- KNOW THAT YOU HAVE TO TREAT EXPLOSIVES WITH A REVERENT RESPECT AT ALL TIMES.

To obtain explosives, most departments already have a system and supplier in place for purchasing military explosives and commercial explosives. Military explosives will always be kept in stock by the bomb techs, so a good supply will be always on hand and the bomb techs are usually eager to help EDD handlers keep a continuous and fresh supply of military style explosives such as C-4, Primasheet flexible

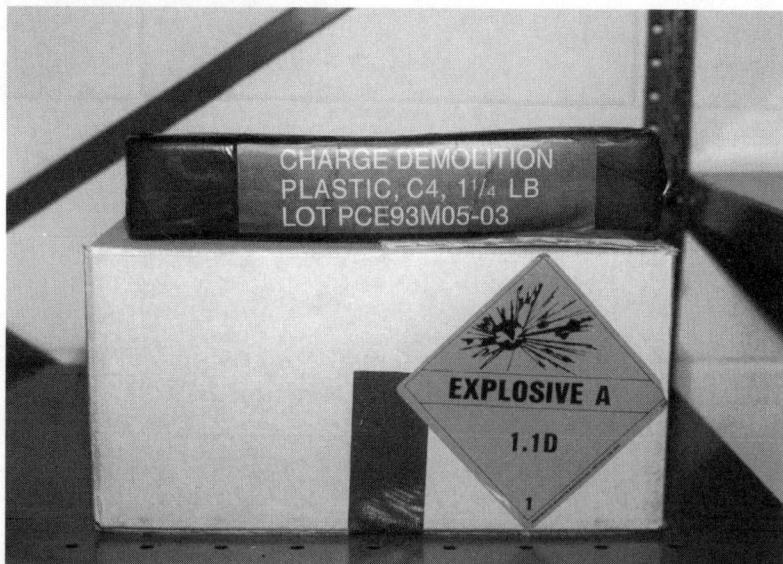

Know your explosives, and above all else, treat them with respect!

explosives or Semtex (if available). To obtain commercial explosives, find a responsible and knowledgeable contact with a commercial explosives dealer. If you live in an area where there is industry that uses an extreme amount of explosives for their work, like the oil industry here in Alberta, you will have an easy time obtaining explosives. However, if you live in an area where there is little of these types of industries, then you are going to have a difficult time obtaining a ready and inexpensive supply of explosives. If you have to obtain military explosives, they cannot be obtained through any source in Canada other than the military or through the Royal Canadian Mounted Police, Bomb Data Center, Ottawa, Ontario.

Most major police departments do have a bomb squad and in order to obtain explosives, you have to have a Licence For Temporary Magazine File Number, obtained through Natural Resources Canada, Explosives Regulatory Division. In the U.S., I don't know what the regulatory division is, but as well as a Federal Agency, there may also be a State Agency that has to be contacted. For our American EDD handlers to obtain precise information, talk to your bomb techs and I know they will help you out. In any event, EDD handlers can either obtain explosives on their bomb techs' existing licence, or they will have to apply to the proper agency for a Temporary Magazine Licence. THIS IS VERY IMPORTANT.

Training with Explosives

For training purposes, I believe that every name brand of explosive should be obtained, listed and placed into your magazines. There does not have to be a large amount of each explosive, but there should always be enough to use for training purposes and enough to be used for certifications. There are those of us who believe that training need only be done with the common explosive elements: RDX, PETN, TNT, NG, Amm. Nit. and Powders. These are the elements that have to be trained on. However, each of these explosive elements comes in a great number of types of explosives (brand names), for example, Primasheet.

Primasheet, I was told, is basically a PETN-based flexible sheet explosive. However, Primasheet comes in two specific types: Primasheet 1000 and Primasheet 2000. Now I will explain where this leads to problems. You may go up to your bomb tech and say, "I want a PETN-based explosive to train the dog on." Your bomb tech then gives you a pound or two of Primasheet. He says, "This is PETN." Be careful here, because you may not be training your dog on PETN. Why? Because Primasheet 1000 is a water- and moisture-proof PETN-based flexible sheet explosive, while Primasheet 2000 is a water- and moisture-proof <u>RDX-based</u> flexible sheet explosive, 88% Cyclo, trimethylene and trinitramine. There is a distinct difference between the two. Be careful. Know what you are training with.

Another PETN based commercial explosive is 1/2 lb., 1 lb. and 2 lb. soup can-shaped explosives. It is a fantastic form of PETN to train the dogs on. They are compact and solid and are easy to hide. These explosives are used for surface charges by seismic crews. I always like to keep a good stock of these, especially if it is hard to obtain other types of PETN explosive.

C-4, too, comes in different mixtures. The C-4 used for military purposes is different from that used for commercial purposes. The military style C-4 comes in one and a quarter pound bricks, while the commercial C-4 comes in one ounce capsules. Commercial C-4 is very pliable, while the military C-4 is not so pliable. Another aspect of C-4 is that you have to practice or train with C-4 in two ways. First, train the dogs on the C-4 out of its green wrap. Let the dog get to know the RDX. The second thing to do is to train the dogs on the C-4 still encased in its wrap. Believe this or not, but there will be a distinct difference in the dogs' indications. I have found that unless the dog is trained on the unwrapped C-4, it will have a great deal of difficulty indicating the wrapped C-4. Once the dog has been introduced to both, there is no problem. However, if you just train the dogs on C-4 chunks taken out of the wrapper, you will have problems with most dogs. My suggestion is to try and if there is a noticeable problem, help them deal with it. If you do try it, place a brick or two of C-4 inside of a clothes-filled suitcase and in another, place the same amount inside but without the wrappers.

Ammonium Nitrate is perhaps the most commonly used explosive ingredient anywhere in the world. This explosive has to be made in large bulk units at mine locations and is mixed with diesel fuel. This called AN FO and is a mixture of 94% Ammonium Nitrate and 6% fuel oil. It is smelly and oily. If you feel you must train your dog on AN FO, let me give you some really good advice. DON'T! There is only the need to train your dog on the Ammonium Nitrate. Training the dogs specifically on AN FO as you would the other explosives will create a magnitude of problems. First, training a dog on AN FO will more than likely assist you in finding all vehicles that run on diesel.

Why? Because, the AN FO has an overwhelming odor of fuel oil and that is what the dog keys on. Also, there is no container that you can put this stuff in that will keep it from contaminating your hands, clothing and the other explosives. Practice only with the pure Ammonium Nitrate. Once a month or so, get your bomb tech guru to make up a gallon of this mixture to test your dog's ability on it. You will see that there will not be any problems.

Other forms of Ammonium Nitrate based explosive that I like to use are the Magnafracs. The Magnafrac most common here in Alberta is Magnafrac 3000. It is safe and comes in long sticks. It has a shelf life of about a year and then it begins to get hard. In its normal state, it is soft because it is a slurry.

Care must be taken not to break the plastic wrapper or casing as it makes one hell of a good mess.

Perchlorates are very common and cheap explosives used in the U.S. and have made their way up here into Canada because they are less expensive for oil companies and mining companies to use. They are not one of the safer explosives to handle, but at the same time they are not any worse either. REMEMBER, TREAT ALL EXPLOSIVES WITH RESPECT! Perchlorates come in the form of sticks wrapped in wax paper. They do have an odor that dogs need to get used to. So be sure to have them on your list of explosives.

NG-based explosives are extremely potent smelling. Be careful with this explosive, for several reasons. One is that if you are in contact with this explosive for long periods of time, either by handling it or just breathing in the air around it, be prepared for an enormous headache and elevated blood pressure. Handle this explosive with gloves and work with it in well-ventilated areas. Two, because of its very odorous state, NG molecules stay in the area for days or weeks, depending upon how much of the explosive was in the area and for how long. That is why it should not be used in areas such as aircraft and air terminals. There is a good chance that the EVDs will continue to pick up traces of the explosive or become contaminated from it. Three, this explosive should always be stored by itself, otherwise it will contaminate the other explosives.

Slurries are a must to have on your list as well. This is Ammonium Nitrate mixed with TNT explosives used for open pit mining, quarries, etc. So the chances of any of this disappearing into the wrong hands is extremely high because so much of this explosive is used at one time.

TNT is an explosive that is getting harder and harder to train with because it is one of the explosives that is slowly becoming extinct. Nitro-pel is the best form of TNT to train on because it comes in the form of TNT pellets. The bad thing about this form of explosive is that the pellets can easily spill all over the place, making clean up very hard. This explosive can still be obtained, but only through enormous bulk orders from China or the USSR via the U.S. If you can get your hands on it, do it, because it is excellent for training.

Powders are also very important to have on hand for training, either black powder or smokeless powder. Powders are the easiest explosive to obtain without any type of licence or application. Because of such easy accessibility, this is one of the most dangerous explosives and if put together right, can do a lot of damage. There are different strengths of smokeless powders and they should be known. Be careful with powders because static electricity can set this explosive off. It doesn't need much help at all, so train with it wisely.

Be sure to train with small amounts of explosive and extremely large amounts. Ask your contact at the dealership when they are getting large shipments of explosives, so that the dogs can be run by the large amounts. This is important for the dog to sense the overwhelming amount of odor.

Have on hand detonator cord and safety fuse for training. These too are important for the dog to know. Although these have common explosive elements inside, the outside or the wrappings are very much different and it is important for the dog to be able to recognize all of the different scents associated with the cords and fuses. Some of you may be saying that the wrappings are not relevant. But they are, because the odor of the cord eventually becomes one of the factors that create the interest for the dog to investigate the source. I can best compare this to a police department having to retrain on another model of 40 cal. handgun. Isn't one model of 40 cal. the same as another model? If so, why do we not just put the newer model into our holsters and go on about our business? The answer is because there are slight differences between the two guns and therefore we require retraining and continued practice. It is the same with all explosives, no matter how similar they are. There is that ever so little difference of a particular brand or type that may cause a dog to leave the hide because the team never practiced on it. Always be prepared. Never take things for granted. Find out for yourself.

Identification of Explosives

Common Names and Descriptions

Safety Fuse

Black or white 1/4 inch cord that normally burns inside.

Usually has black powder in the center. It burns at 12 inches per 40 seconds.

Detonator Cord

Comes in many colors. Very stable explosive which contains either PETN or RDX. This type of explosive detonates at speeds of 4 miles or 24 000 feet/second.

Boosters

These are copper or plastic casings containing PETN and are used for increasing the intensity of an explosion from a detonation.

Dynamite

This is tightly wrapped in heavy brown paper, usually containing a Nitroglycerin base (NG base) with assorted materials. Dynamite comes in many types:

1) Nitroglycerin straight dynamite has a very low detonation temperature. Forms explosive salts with metals and is soluble in alcohol or acetone. It is very unstable and dangerous. It should be rotated every 30 to 90 days.

2) Ammonia (stumping powders, Stopeite, Blastal and Belite). These are all dynamites that have some of the NG replaced by ammonia nitrate. Used for clearing land.

3) Gelatins (forcites, power fracs, geogels and submagels). These contain nitroglycerin/nitro cellose/sodium nitrate and carbonaceous fuel. Used in seismic, rock and underwater blasting. Has a short shelf life. Forcites that show liquid should be considered dangerous!

4) Ammonia Gelatin (semi-gelatins, Cilgel, Dygel and Xactex). These contain nitroglycerin/nitro cellose/ammonia nitrate and carbonaceous fuel. These explosives are used for general mining and construction.

TNT

Trinitrotoluene, Tolite, Nitro-pel and Pelletol. Found in the form of cast, pressed or prills (spherical pellets). Widely used in military applications (landmines and main charges) and in mining applications (prills for borehole fillers), TNT is one of the moderately insensitive military explosives and cannot be detonated by heat, shocks or friction. It is relatively safe.

Ammonium Nitrate

Prills and slurries. Ingredient of explosives mixtures and dynamite, cratering charges and fertilizer. Ammonium Nitrate is fast becoming the most widely used explosive on the market today and is a common agent with other explosive mixtures. This explosive is becoming prevalent with bombers/terrorists who want to make a big impact.

Nitroglycerin

In its pure state, Nitroglycerin is extremely sensitive to shock, heat and friction. It is a thick liquid like castor oil. Its sensitivity is increased by application of heat. In pure form it is extremely dangerous and unstable, prone to explosion if jarred, overheated or contaminated.

Powders

These are black or grey in color. They are not subject to deterioration and are sensitive to heat and friction.

RDX

Cyclotrimethylene Trinitramine, Cyclonite or Hexogen. It is one of the most powerful explosives and is generally used as a base charge in electric and non-electric blasting caps and commercial booster charges. RDX is the base for C-3 and C-4 military plastic explosives. It is white in color, crystalline, odorless and powdered, much like fine sugar. Its crystals are sensitive to heat, shock and friction. Should any RDX crystals be observed, they should be wetted down and transported in a wet condition. Some of the common explosives with RDX are as follows:

1) Composition "A-3," which is a mixture of RDX and wax used for booster and shaped charges and found usually in the form of pressed tablets. These tablets easily break and I do not recommend them for training.

2) Composition "B" (Cyclotol, Tritolite or Hexolite). Mixture of 60% RDX and 40% TNT. Used for fragmentation bombs, projectiles and grenades.

3) Composition "C-4" (Harrisite). This is a mixture of 91% RDX and 9% non-explosive plasticizer. This is a putty-like material that can be used under water and is high strength, cap-sensitive. Has an excellent shelf life.

PETN

Pentaerythritol Tetranitrate. This is relatively insensitive to detonation by friction or ordinary shocks and therefore is one of the safer explosives to handle. Pure PETN is white in color and is used in detonator cord (det. cord). PETN also comes in other forms of explosives: Sheet PETN, Flex-X or

Detasheet, now called Primasheet. Called Flex-X by the military and Primasheet by commercial sources. It is a mixture of PETN/NC/Plasticizer or PETN/RDX or HMX/Plasticizer. Used as cutting charges on irregular surfaces and metallurgical work and boosters. Primasheet is extremely flexible, waterproof, easily cut, high strength and cap-sensitive.

Power Mex

Hydromex, Powermex, Powergel, Tovex LD and SD, Sak-Pak and Nitrex. These are your slurry/watergel/emulsion explosives. Ingredients are AN/SN solutions plus AN plus sensitizer. Power mex itself is a special formula of metallized (aluminum) cap-sensitive slurry explosive. It is highly resistant to detonation by shock, friction or impact. Has a good shelf-life. Hydromex, on the other hand, is a mixture of Ammonium Nitrate and TNT. Moisture can affect some of the ingredients, otherwise it is a stable product.

AN FO

This is an explosive with a mixture of 94% Ammonium Nitrate and 6% fuel oil. This mixture is usually used for mining where the prills are poured into boreholes. It is usually mixed in bulk and used in large quantities. Care should be taken when using this mixture for training dogs. The fuel oil smell is very strong and continuous training on this mixture may confuse the dog when it approaches diesel engines and fuel tanks. This mixture will also easily contaminate other explosives used for training, therefore, practicing with this mixture should be avoided unless absolutely necessary, and then only by itself.

Explosives Abbreviations

- AN   AMMONIUM NITRATE (also commonly abbreviated Amm. Nit.)
- SN   SODIUM NITRATE
- NG   NITRO GLYCERIN
- EGDN   ETHYLENE GLYCOL DINITRATE
- EGMN   ETHYLENE GLYCOL MONO NITRATE
- MMAN   MONOMETHYLAMINE NITRATE
- NC   NITRO CELLOSE
- PETN   PENTAERYTHRITE TETRA NITRATE
- TNT   TRINITRO TOLUENE

- DNT   DINITROTULUENE
- RDX   CYCLO TRIMETHYLENE TRINITRAMINE
- BP   BLACK POWDER

Explosives Compositions

- A-3   RDX, beeswax
- C-3 and C-4   RDX, plasticizer
- DM-12   PETN, coal oil and soap
- Dynamites   (Forcite, Geogel, Powerfrag, etc.) NG, EGDN, NC, AN, SN.
- Powermex   AN, SN, EGMN.
- Tovex   AN, SN, MMAN (guar gum, gel agent)
- Amex/Amite   AN, fuel oil (most are known as AN FO mixes)
- Nitropel   TNT
- Pentolite   PETN, TNT
- Detonator Cords   PETN, Some also contain RDX, TNT or a PETN/TNT mixture
- Primasheet   PETN and plasticizer or RDX
- Safety Fuse   (white, yellow, orange, black, military olive drab) PC core
- Black Powder   SN, sulphur, charcoal, graphite
- Smokeless Powder   single base/NC; double base/NC, NG
- Blasting Caps   lead sulphinate, lead, azide, PETN or RDX
- Fireworks   BP, nitrates, chlorates

The above data is always changing in name and in makeup. Today's explosives are becoming less sensitive but offering a bigger bang. However, that being said, more explosives than ever are being used today and as a result, you can be guaranteed that more and more of the explosives disappear and go unreported. This is one of the reasons I am telling you, as EDD handlers, to know your explosives. Know what they look like and know their names and their contents.

Carrying the explosives to and from your training sites should be done with the use of small ammo boxes. These are sturdy and you can get different sizes of ammo boxes to suit your needs. However, there is always the problem of placing out the explosives once you are at the venue. What is the best way of doing this? I am not sure that there is one. Care must always be taken not to get the explosive contaminated or to contaminate the hiding spot. I, and probably the majority of other trainers and handlers, have used plastic containers with tight lids to keep the small amounts of training explosives in.

We would then just set out the whole container in the hiding spot. The bad thing about this is that sometimes they were left behind, even though they were marked in the notebook, for whatever reason. I always suggest that the explosive be taken right out of its container and then placed into the hiding spot, with the container going back into the ammo box. Now, when you open the ammo box, you see all of the empty plastic containers and you go about looking for the right explosive hide to be placed back into its container.

There was a problem with this too until I saw what the RCMP dog handlers do. The problem was what to do with the loose (flaked or prilled) explosives. You can't just put a loose pile of powder or prills into a drawer. It is messy and the people using the desk or locker don't appreciate it. The RCMP use ladies nylon stockings. Their explosives were placed inside of nylons and it works great. When your wife or girlfriend gets a run in her pantyhose, make sure she doesn't throw them away. Wash them in soapless hot water, spin dry them and then air dry them. Just use the leg part of the pantyhose, because it is the sheerest and will allow more of the explosive scent through. Because this material stretches and forms to the explosive, you have to cut the right amount off. In order to do this I cut the foot off and discard it and then knot it at the end. I then cut the top of the legs where they meet the panty part of the hose and discard the panty part. I then cut the legs into pieces of 12 inches or more, depending how much explosive you wish to put in or how long some of the sticks are. Place the explosive inside and tie a knot at both ends. For the loose explosives, a pound or two can be placed inside very easily. But for these, I double up the hose so that there are two layers holding the loose prills or powders and have both ends knotted. It is doubled up just in case the nylon is snagged while it is full of powder. Doubling it up will prevent the powders or prills from spilling in such cases. In order to place the explosive into its hiding place, you only have to pick it up by the tied end with your fingertips and set it in place. I am sure that most of you are already doing this, but for those of you who aren't, it's a great system.

Amounts to Keep on Hand for Training Purposes

There is no particular amount that is recommended for training purposes. However, I do have my own preference for amounts to have on hand for training. I will list them and for your preferences as a trainer, you decide how much you require. Whether or not some of the explosives are related in content, I still have them to practice on. I advise everyone to do the same. Here is a list a trainer can follow for his/her own purposes:

TYPE	MINIMUM AMOUNTS	MAXIMUM AMOUNTS
C-4 (military)	2 blocks (2 1/2 lbs.)	4 blocks (5 lbs.)
C-4 (commercial)	32 oz.	32 oz.
Dynamite	6/40% forcite 6/75% forcite	10/40% forcite 10/75% forcite
Powermex	6 sticks	10 sticks
Detonator Cord	4 feet	6 feet
Safety Fuse	4 feet	6 feet
Hydromex	5 lbs.	10 lbs.
Powders (smokeless and black)	2 lbs. of each	4 lbs. of each
Perchlorates	6 sticks	10 sticks
Pentex 16	6 pieces	10 pieces
Magnafrac 3000	6 sticks	10 sticks
Nitropel	6 lbs.	12 lbs.
Ammonium Nitrate	6 lbs.	12 lbs.
Geogel	6 pieces	10 pieces
Primasheet	2 lbs.	6 lbs.

This list is not the gospel. I just tried to make a list that covers everything that may come up and I dislike surprises. I like to be ready and so should all trainers and handlers.

Common Ingredients of Explosives

There are many different items around the workshop and house that you can most likely find in explosives. I list these for your information, because there may be a chance that a dog may become very interested in an element similar to that used in explosives and want to confirm. It is a distant chance that it could happen, but nonetheless, it could happen. Here is a list of common ingredients found in explosives:

Plasticizer

Websters dictionary – one that plasticizes; a chemical added especially to rubbers and resins to impart flexibility, workability or stretchability.

Potassium

Potash – a silver white, soft, light, low-melting, univalent, metallic element of the alkali metal group that occurs abundantly in nature, especially combined in minerals.

Potassium Chloride – a crystalline salt occurring as a mineral and in natural waters and used as a fertilizer (KCl).

Potassium Chlorate – a crystalline salt that is used as an oxidizing agent in matches, fireworks and explosives ($KClO_3$).

Potassium Hydroxide – used for making soap.

Potassium Nitrate – used in gunpowder, medicines and preserving meats.

Potassium Sulphate – used in fertilizer.

Sodium Nitrate (sodium NA)

A crystallizing salt used as fertilizer, as an oxidizing agent and in curing meat.

Ammonium Nitrate (AN)

A colorless crystalline salt used in explosives and fertilizers.

Wax

Of mineral origin, consisting usually of higher hydrocarbons.

Charcoal

A dark or black porous carbon prepared from vegetable or animal substances.

Aluminum

A bluish silver-white, malleable, dactile, light, trivalent, metallic element with good electrical and thermal conductivity, light reflectivity and resistance to oxidation, that is the most abundant metal in the earth's crust occurring always in combination.

Sulfur or Sulphur

A non-metallic element that occurs either free or combined, especially in sulfides and sulfates; it is a constituent of proteins, exists in several allotropic forms, including yellow orthorhombic crystals. Resembles oxygen chemically but is less active and more acidic, and is used especially in the chemical and paper industries, and in medicines.

Fuel Oil

An oil that is used for fuel and that usually has a higher flash point than kerosene.

Ethylene Glycol

Ethylene is a colorless, flammable, gaseous, unsaturated hydrocarbon found in coal gas or obtained by pyrolysis of petroleum hydrocarbons. A bivalent hydrocarbon derived from ethane. Ethylene Glycol is a thick liquid alcohol used especially in anti-freeze. Used to keep some explosives from freezing.

The Internet

As we all know, technology has made it easier to access knowledge. So much so that it has created serious problems by jeopardizing public safety. I am talking about today's teens (among others) and access to information on the Internet that shows them how to make explosives, explosive devices and so on. Some of the ingredients listed on the Internet are easily obtained from the grocery store, gas stations and from their own homes.

Several incidents across Canada, and I am sure the U.S. as well, have arisen regarding bombs made up of mixtures of gasoline and other chemicals. If there seems to be a sharp rise in these situations, DO NOT INVESTIGATE WITH YOUR DOG/DO NOT TRAIN YOUR DOG ON THESE TYPES OF BOMBS. These are bombs that are meant to explode due to a chemical reaction forming a gas. Some of these could have very corrosive chemicals or have frags inside. The value of searching for these bombs, that more than likely will harm both the dog and handler, is not worth it. That is why bomb techs have mechanical robots. Chemical devices should never be investigated with a dog.

Some Points of Interest

- Handle explosives with care at all times.
- Try to wear rubber gloves or use plastic tongs to prevent contamination and/or for health reasons.
- Use small quantities for training but vary the amounts from time to time. However, on occasion, use amounts of 100 lbs. or more to acclimatize the dogs to large amounts.
- Rotate explosives every two to three months if it is possible. If deterioration is noticed, then replace immediately.
- Do not train with blasting caps.
- Store and transport all explosives in approved magazines.
- Remember where you place or set out the hides.
- Always train with a #2 man. It is called the buddy system.
- Always do a call with the whole team.
- Always give good instructions when someone else is setting out the hides.
- Detail all hides, what explosives and where, in your notebook and training manual.
- Detail entry log located in the magazine, date out/date in and initial.
- Never leave the hides unattended.
- Don't contaminate the explosives.
- Don't let the dog contaminate the explosives.
- Don't let the dog at the hides.

Radio Transmitting

One of the basic rules that we are taught when we are approaching a threat situation is to turn off our radios (this also includes cell phones, pagers, etc.). Although I haven't been able to find any concrete proof that radio waves from a police radio have caused an explosion, I do believe that it can and probably has happened. There always has been great concern that anyone transmitting on their radios while close to the scene can possibly set off the device; hence the practice of turning off the radios. I always have and always will teach my students the practice of turning off the radios and telling everyone else in the area to do the same.

The same applies to the commercial aspect of blasting. When blasting in the vicinity of a radio transmitter, a charge shall not be loaded, primed or fired. The transmitter power dictates the distance, i.e.,

● For transmitter power of 5 to 25 watts, there will be a minimum distance of 35 meters from the blasting area. For transmitter power of 25 000 to 50 000 watts, there will be a minimum distance 1525 meters from the blasting area.

● A radio transmitter in a vehicle at or near the blasting area will have the power switch in the OFF position at all times when there are detonators outside their magazine or above the ground.

● When you arrive at the scene with your dog to assess the situation, there is no doubt that zone personnel have already used their radios close by or at the scene and have not caused the device to go off; however, rather than becoming complacent and uncaring, leave your radio in the car. Turn everything to the OFF position and make sure that zone or patrol personnel do likewise. Remember that it's your life and maybe the lives of others that you may save by not using your radio.

PLAY IT SAFE, NOT SORRY !

Storage and Transportation

Magazines

1) Use only magazines that are designed and constructed in accordance with the standards of Federal, State or Provincial laws. In Canada these standards are set out by the National Building Code of Canada.

2) Adhere to the regulations regarding placement of magazines. The magazines can only be situated within a given minimum distance from buildings and services such as gas and electric.

3) Ideally, the magazine should be inside of a building, out of the elements. It has been found that dynamite deteriorates rapidly in a magazine that is located in an open field exposed to the sun.

4) Keep the magazine locked at all times.

5) Use proper safety measures when transporting explosives for training purposes.

   a) Use one explosive per training session and carry only what you need. This will keep explosives from being cross-contaminated, and prevents large amounts of explosives from being transported unnecessarily.

   b) Always transport in a magazine or in a proper military ammo can for safety's sake and to eliminate contamination odors from you/dog/vehicle. Don't be apprehensive about having 6 or 8 boxes that are marked for what they will carry.

   Be a wise trainer and/or supervisor. Know what the laws are concerning the transportation of explosives. It is the handlers who have to transport the explosives when they are training and it is they who will pay the price criminally if they break a law concerning the transportation of explosives. Don't be like one canine supervisor who had made up his mind that there would not be any magazine placed in the canine vehicle. He was going to get them a trailer to haul the explosives around the city. VERY BAD MOVE. Anyways, he was convinced to do otherwise once I showed him the law, which clearly states that explosives can only be moved within a vehicle, and not in a detachable unit.

Inventories/Log Sheets

A careful inventory must be kept of all receipts of blasting explosives and detonators to a magazine and every issue from it. In this case, we do not need to concern ourselves with blasting caps. Care must be taken to ensure that stocks do not exceed the licence limits for the magazine as the law provides for a penalty when limits are exceeded.

Inventory control sheets indicating explosive in/explosive out must be in all magazines and filled in each time the explosives are moved in or out. An example is:

Magazine No. _____		Explosive Limit Weight _____ kg			
Date	Brand Name	Stock Used			Signature
	Explosive & Weight	Wt Out	Wt In	Balance	
30/07/96	ICI-Nitro-gel 20 kg	2 kg	2 kg	20 kg	Cst. S.S.
15/08/96	ICI-Nitro-gel 20 kg	20 kg	destroyed	0 kg	Cst. S.S.

It is best to use weights when itemizing your explosives for training, the reason being that you may not wish to use a whole stick of Geogel, for example, or a whole bag of Nitropel. Instead you may only wish to use a 1/4 stick of Geogel (.600kg) rather than 2 kg, or 1200 grams of Nitropel rather than a 50 kg bag. Therefore, acquire two scales, one for grams and the other for kilograms.

It is a good idea when getting your explosives, commercial explosives especially, that you break them down into different weights suitable for training. After you have completed this, mark your weights corresponding to specific explosives on your magazine inventory sheet. A lot of the explosives used today are the slurries. DO NOT CUT THEM INTO SMALLER SIZES! They get too messy. Leave them in their manufactured state.

Type 6 Magazine (bin, box or cupboard)

The Type 6 magazine is the most commonly used magazine for transporting and storing smaller amounts of explosives for training purposes. It is also used as a day box for overnight storing of explosives.

Uses

Magazines built to this standard may be licensed or unlicensed magazines for storage of small quantities of blasting explosives or detonators and must conform to all applicable laws. For additional security, the magazines may be placed in a suitable building that is also security locked.

Storage

The maximum storage quantity for a Type 6 magazine is 10 cases of blasting explosive (250 kg) or 10 000 detonators.

Day Box

When not in use as a magazine, it may be used as a transportation container or as a day box under the following conditions:

1) A transportation container may be carried in a truck cargo box, during which time it shall be locked and otherwise conform to all applicable regulations.

When used as a transportation container in the open cargo space of a vehicle, provisions must be made to maintain separation between the two to prevent communication of an explosion or a fire.

2) A day box may be used on a work site where there is a requirement to safeguard explosives at the place of use. A day box denotes an unlicensed facility that is not used for storage.

Size and Storage Capacity

The internal volume shall not exceed 0.6 cubic metre. This volume is sufficient for the storage of 10 cases of most blasting explosives, allowing sufficient empty space for handling and air circulation. For lesser quantities, the volume may be reduced.

First-Aid and Health

Ingestion of Explosives

This of great importance. Be sure that your vet knows the effects of the specific explosives should your dog swallow some. Also be sure that your vet has the correct treatments immediately available in case the dog swallows an explosive. It is important that the clinic is ready to immediately proceed with these treatments.

Of course, the safest and surest way of preventing the dogs from ingesting is to be sure the dogs cannot get at the hides. Malinois come to mind as the sneakiest dogs I have seen that can scoff up a piece of explosive and swallow it. Trying to get a Malinois to drop it out of their mouth usually comes with a price attached to it: the handler gets chewed up. So keep explosive hides out of reach.

In most cases ingestion of explosives is extremely dangerous and requires the attention of a vet. Field treatments will not help unless the other steps to be followed up are close at hand. Should your vet not have immediate information, this little bit should help out.

TNT Ingestion

1) Signs – Nitrate poisoning.*
2) Treatment:
   O Induce vomiting** followed by a good washing or rinsing out of the system (gastric lavage).
   O Examine for Methaemoglobinaemia***
   O Then the dog needs to be placed on a special diet.****
   O Examine blood samples for RBC dyscrasia and hemoglobin levels at weekly intervals for six to eight weeks after.

C-4 Ingestion

1) Signs – hyperexcitability, convulsions or changes in the behavior.
2) Treatment:
   O Control the convulsions by administering 10mg of Valium intravenously (subcutaneously). Repeat at 3 to 4 hour intervals.

○ Induce vomiting (emesis).**
○ Examine for Methaemoglobinaemia***
○ Place the dog on a special diet.****

Smokeless Powder Ingestion (Without the NG Base)

1) Signs – Considered non-toxic.
2) Treatment:
   ○ Induce vomiting (emesis)** followed by a gastric lavage (good internal rinsing).

Smokeless Powder With NG Base

1) Signs – Same as dynamite.
2) Treatment
   ○ Induce vomiting (emesis)**
   ○ Hasten elimination and protect irritated mucosa by administering 60cc of mineral oil per oz.
   ○ Examine for Methaemoglobinaemia.***
   ○ Feed a bland diet with high levels of all vitamins.
   * Gastritis, methaemoglobinaemia, toxic hepatitis, aplastic and hemolytic anemia, cataract formation, dermatitis, CNS, cardiac irregularities and urinary tract irritation have been reported.
   ** Administer 0.04 mg of apomorphine hydrochloride per pound of body weight intravenously or two tablespoons of salt per oz.
   *** Chocolate brown colored blood is an indication of methaemoglobinaemia. Spectrophotometric analysis of the blood should be a routine procedure for the first several days post-exposure. A 25% or greater concentration of methaemoglobin should be treated with 2% methylene blue, 1 ml per five pounds of body weight. I/V repeated if necessary.
   **** Feed a diet high in calcium and carbohydrates (i.e., milk). Administer high levels of B complex vitamins and Vitamin D.

As you can see, these are very complex administrations of procedures and medicines. These would be very difficult to do in the field.

Health of the Dogs

Health of the dogs is very simple. Feed them with healthy food and there are enough of them out there. But most of all, the best health ingredient to a healthy searcher is to exercise the dogs continuously. Run them, run them and run them.

This is the best exercise you can give to a detector dog. Taking it one step further, it is probably very healthy for us handlers as well. A fit dog is a sharp dog.

Just how effective and efficient your dog will work in an environment that is hot, dry and enclosed will be partly determined by its diet and exercise routine.

Laws to Know

I am not going to get into detail of our laws or the American laws. These are things that if you wish to get convictions, you should already know. By time I have this book written and published, one or two of the laws will have been changed. So for this little chapter I will just add a few more laws or rules to what I have already mentioned throughout the book.

The day to day transportation of explosives by anyone, falls under the jurisdiction of Canada Transportation of Dangerous Goods Act and in the U.S. under the United States Department of Transportation.

If you are transporting in excess of 25 kg, then your vehicle must be appropriately signed, the words EXPLOSIVES printed in luminous paint in letters not less than 15cm in height on a contrasting background.

Placards are to be placed on all four sides of the vehicle if you are transporting more than 25 kg of explosive.

If you are involved in an accident while transporting explosives, an additional accident report must be submitted to Transport Canada.

Know the following:

- The mishandling of explosives for whatever purpose falls under the jurisdiction of the Criminal Code or the Explosives Act, R,S 1985, c.E-17 amended by 1989, C3.
- Crimes with intent to hurt, or related to the cause of death to others fall under sections within the Criminal Code.
- Crimes of prohibited activities and offences of the commercial or industrial nature, i.e., unsafe storage or endangering persons through unsafe transportation practices, fall under the Explosives Act and Regulations.

Glossary of Terms and Acronyms

- ARMING

    The act of installing a detonator into or onto an explosive device, the crimping of a blasting cap onto the detonating card in a perforating gun.

- AUTHORIZED EXPLOSIVE

    An explosive that has been successfully tested as per the Explosives Act (Canada) and subsequently declared an authorized explosive by the Chief Inspector.

- CARBONACEOUS

    Pertaining to or yielding carbon.

- CONFIRMATION

    Confirmation is the final step of indicating the presence of source. The confirmation or THE SIT, the verification or corroboration of evidence, in this case, the scent cone of explosives odor.

- CURSORY SEARCH or SCAN

    Is the act by which the EDD quickly moves ahead through the search area in order to locate an explosive device or a hide of explosives within the immediate search area without the handler by its side or without completing a systematic search routine.

- DEFLAGRATE

    A capsule or case of such strength and construction which contains an explosive of the fulminate class in such quantity that the explosives of one capsule will communicate the explosion to the other capsules. A blasting cap, an electrical blasting cap or other like devices used to detonate explosives.

- ELECTRIC BLASTING CAP

    A shell containing a charge of detonating compound, designed to be fired by an electric current.

- **EXPLOSIVE CARTRIDGE**

  A case of paper, metal or plastic which contains an explosive compound or mixture.

- **EXPLOSIVES**

  Any substance that is made, manufactured or used to produce an explosion, detonation or a pyrotechnic effect. Examples are: gun powders, propellant powders, blasting agents, dynamite, detonating cord, lead oxide detonators, ammunition, rockets, fireworks, firework compositions, safety flares and other signals.

  Any chemical compound or mixture manufactured, compounded or mixed for the purpose of causing a sudden generation of high pressure gases by fire, friction, impact, percussion or detonation, including but not limited to gun powder, blasting powder, nitroglycerin, gun cotton, dynamite, blasting gelatin, gelignite, fulminate of mercury or other metals.

- **FALSE SIT**

  False sits are usually an act of frustration on the dog's part. The dog's frustration is usually caused by: the handler moving too slow, the dog has been worked for a period of time longer than it should have and is becoming too tired, was not properly run and has to relieve itself or is ill. With the exception of the illness, the rest are common causes to false sitting. It is basically how the dog handles frustration or pressure.

- **FULMINATE**

  To explode or detonate violently an explosively unstable compound.

- **HB**

  This is the hide box that contains the explosive during the box searching routines.

- **HIDES**

  These are the different amounts and types of explosives that are set out in such manner that only the scent of the explosive is exposed to the dog. A hide is often hidden in a manner that would be similar to that of a bomber or terrorist.

- **IGNITION SOURCE**

  Includes heat, sparks, flames, static electricity and friction.

- **INDICATIONS**

This is the act of suggesting or demonstrating through specific body or physical actions that point out the presence of the source is nearby. The specific body or physical actions of the dog are such things as a fresh awakening to life or excitement, a wagging tail, a perky posture, ears erect and ahead and a closed mouth and determined sniffing. This is the act of finding the scent cone and working it to its source.

● INTEREST

It is when the dog is induced or persuaded to focus its attention towards an item or object due to a pungent odor other than an explosive odor. The attention is usually short lived and there are no noticeable changes in the dog's physical characteristics other than taking the time to sniff. Interest is often mistaken for indications.

● MAGAZINE

Any building, storehouse, structure or place in which any explosive is kept or stored. Does not include the following:

1) A vehicle conveying authorized explosives in accordance with the Explosives Act.
2) A place in which an authorized amount of explosives is kept for private use and not for sale.
3) A place in which an authorized amount of explosives is kept for sale.
4) A place at which the blending or assembling of the in-explosive component parts of an authorized explosive is allowed.

● MASS EXPLOSION

An explosion that effects the entire load virtually instantaneously (en masse explosion).

● NET (NET EXPLOSIVE QUANTITY)

The weight of explosive material only, not including liners, casings or other packaging.

● NITRIC ACID

A colorless, heavy oil liquid which has a very strong capability for attacking vegetable and animal substances as well as most metals.

About half the Nitric Acid produced is used for making explosives. It is also used in fertilizers, plastics, lacquers, photographic films and dyes. Small amounts of nitric acid are formed during lightning storms, which breaks down into nitrates essential for the growth of vegetation.

● OXIDER

A chemical which supplies its own oxygen and helps other combustible material burn more readily.

● PERCHLORATE

An acid forming a syrupy liquid that is very explosive.

● PERFORATING

The use of explosive charges to create holes in a well bore so that fluids from the formations may flow more readily into the well bore.

● PRIMER

The detonator when attached to an explosive charge.

● SAFETY FUSE

A fuse for blasting that burns and does not explode, does not contain its own means of ignition and contains an explosive in such quantity that the burning of such fuse will not communicate laterally with the other fuses. It consists of a train of black powder tightly wrapped and enclosed in a series of textiles and waterproof materials.

● SCENT CONE

This is the pattern of scent or odor as it emanates from the source. The shape of the pattern from source outward is approximately cone shaped. At the source or the hide, the width of the cone is as wide as the hide itself. As the scent or odor emanates from the source, the width of the scent or odor becomes wider. The farther from the source, the wider it gets, hence the shape of a cone. It is during the cursory searches that the dog enters into the widest portion of the scent cone. The dog finds the exact place of the source by crossing back and forth or zig zagging until it reaches the narrowest point of the scent cone, at which time it follows with its nose to the source. A scent cone either falls or travels along a surface.

● SOAK TIME

This is the allotted time for the odor or scent of the explosive to emanate enough to create a scent cone so that the dog is able to indicate and confirm the source or the hide. The length of soak time is pre-determined by such factors as temperature, venue, size of hide and type of explosive.

- SOURCE

  This is the cause or the heart of the scent/odor. It is the hide itself.

- TYPE 6 MAGAZINE

  A container constructed to certain specifications, used in any industry for the separate storage of explosives or detonators.

- TYPE 7 MAGAZINE

  A temporary, portable, two-compartment magazine of a design approved by the Chief Inspector of Explosives, appointed under the provisions of the Explosives Act (Canada).

Selected Bibliography

Dangerous Goods, Systems and Supplies Ltd., 1992, *Guide to Canadian Transportation of Dangerous Goods Act and Regulations*, mini version 1992.

Energy, Mines and Resources Canada, *Explosives Regulations*, C.R.C., c.599.

Energy, Mines and Resources Canada, *Explosives Act*, R., S., 1985, C.E-17 amended by 1989, C.3.

Energy, Mines and Resources Canada – Explosives Branch, Supplement Canada Gazette, Part I 1992, *List of Authorized Explosives*.

Energy, Mines and Resources Canada – Explosives Branch, 1985, *Blasting and Detonators, Storage, Possession, Transportation, Destruction and Sale*.

Energy, Mines and Resources Canada – Explosives Branch, 1982, *Magazine Standards for Blasting Explosives and Detonators*.

Explosives Limited, 1992, *Perforating Products and Wireline Equipment*.

Royal Canadian Mounted Police Training and Development Branch, Ottawa, Canada, *Course Training Standard*, Dog Handler Training Course.

Department of Defence, Department of the Air Force, Air Education and Training Command, *State of Work Standard*, Lackland, AFB, Texas, U.S.A.

The Police Officer's Manual, 14th ed. – 1997, Gary P. Rodrigues.

The Pocket Criminal Code, 1996 – Carswell.

AGMV Marquis

MEMBER OF SCABRINI MEDIA

Quebec, Canada
2003